# superfoods
# HONEY

*by*
**Inara Hasanali**

**HEALTH HARMONY**

*An imprint of*
**B. Jain Publishers (P) Ltd.**
USA — Europe — India

**Disclaimer**

Any information given in this book is not intended to be taken as a replacement for medical advice. Any person with a condition requiring medical attention should consult a qualified practitioner or therapist.

superfoods - Honey

First Edition: 2013
1st Impression: 2013

All rights reserved. No part of this book may be reproduced, stored in a retrieval system or transmitted, in any form or by any means, mechanical, photocopying, recording or otherwise, without any prior written permission of the publisher.

© with the author

Published by Kuldeep Jain for

*An imprint of*
**B. JAIN PUBLISHERS (P) LTD.**
1921/10, Chuna Mandi, Paharganj, New Delhi 110 055 (INDIA)
Tel.: +91-11-4567 1000 • Fax: +91-11-4567 1010
Email: info@bjain.com • Website: **www.bjain.com**

Printed in India by
J.J. Offset Printers

ISBN: 978-81-319-1135-8

# PREFACE

'Honey'… saying the word aloud or thinking about it generally brings a smile on my face as I'm sure it must to yours. Honey is a word that almost involuntarily brings a feeling of pleasantness when one reads it, refers to it or says it aloud. Whether one refers to a beloved as honey or thinks of the delicious food 'honey', the experience is always of sweetness; whether it is a feeling or a sensory taste.

Honey bees have existed on our planet from the Neolithic Age around ten to twenty million years before humankind. Humankind is indeed a fortunate species to benefit from nature's innumerable bounties, one of the better among them being honey.

Humankind, as an alchemist, has never been able to turn base metal into gold through years and years of striving. However, the small and studious honeybee has managed to turn nectar from flowers into liquid gold or honey.

Initially, humankind may have foraged individually for honey, with great personal risk including the fact that they could slip from climbing hollow trees and rock crevices to reach wild honey as well as being stung by honey bees. Today, we are fortunate to have apiarists or bee producers or individuals harvesting over 2 billion pounds of honey every year for our consumption. This honey is sourced from around 50 million cultivated and wild hives.

Researchers have proved that honey bees originated in Africa. Today bees spread their wings worldwide. We can find bees everywhere except at the extreme North and South Pole.

A magnificent gift from nature, I hope that humankind learns to appreciate the honey bee and to judiciously use the excellent products it so generously has made available to us, especially honey, without harming the habitats of the bees by exploitation or harming the basic constitution of the bee by dosing it with antibiotics or feeding it with sugar and water to increase yield. Overexploitation in any way, of this wonderful little insect that shares the bounties of our planet so generously with us, is something we should avoid at all costs.

**Inara Hasanali**

# ACKNOWLEDGEMENTS

I am extremely grateful to the Almighty and the Universe for all the blessings bestowed on me.

I am also grateful for the support of my parents Soghra and Hasanali, my siblings, my sisters who are my greatest ever support – Yasmin, Nasreen, Parveen and my brother Sajjad. I also thank the numerous uncles, aunties, brothers-in-law, cousins, nieces and nephews for their encouragement.

I thank the entire team at B Jain Publishing Group, especially, Mr Nitin Jain, Dr Geeta Rani Arora, the entire editorial team including Ms Somomita Taneja, Mr Sanjay Kumar, Ms Manpreet Kaur and Mr Vijesh Chahal, the illustrators and each and every individual who has been involved with and helped in publishing this book. A special thanks to the gracious Ms Nina Kochhar for being kind enough to introduce me to my publishers. I also thank Massimo Brogi for having confidence in my writing skills and for commissioning my first ever paid article on food many years ago.

Many friends have always stood by me but some of them have overextended themselves to support me through this book. I extend my thanks to all of them. A deeply felt grateful thanks to Bob Thompson for his quiet and constant support for being there at all the different phases I have gone through writing this book. This book is specially dedicated to him as I believe that his nature is as sweet if not sweeter than honey. Sherwin Rodrigues' encouragement and support is something I'm beginning to take for granted. Words are insufficient to convey my deep felt gratitude to Shamsah Dhala for her unconditional support and excellent editing that has definitely improved my standard of writing. I also thank Sherwin Rodrigues and Karishma Lakdawalla for having sincerely read the manuscript and Padma S for reading part of the manuscript. I thank Sarfaraz Lakdawalla for his ability to help me look positively at the progress of my writing career.

I also acknowledge the support of both old friends and new, some of them being Husnara Alim, Alice Squire, Samantha Harvey, Santhi MKS, Kalai Selvi Saravanan, Shakila Murad Virani, Bindu Dinesh, Prameela Yogeshwaran, Peter Brunton, Omprakash Kashinath Mishra, Mayur Vora, Keith Pinto, Kaushik Patel, Shailaja Suresh Kumar, Lata Gopati, Suganthi Soundar, Avinash Subramaniam, Vidya Mani, Nadia Makhani, Dimple Mohamed, Nadya Javed and Ameena Pirani.

I would also like to thank all the researchers, writers, apiarists, chefs, cooks, beauticians, chemists, doctors, healers and lovers of nature who have shared their knowledge and experiences with me.

God bless all of you.

**Inara Hasanali**

## PUBLISHER'S NOTE

We know that honey is among the most valuable natural foods that nature has blessed mankind with. Hindu mythology gives it the honour of a – 'Panchamrit' – sacred food. It is a natural food with the taste of divine bliss.

But, people today have made, junk food so much a part of their lifestyle that they hardly care to notice the natural rich foods present on the planet.

The book **Honey** is an attempt to deepen the understanding about the goodness of this ultimate food – Honey.

All in all, most of us should realise the advantages of this nectarian food and not let its presence be futile in this universe.

We thank Inara Hasanali for providing us with this excellent work so that the common man's awareness and use of honey can be enhanced.

**Kuldeep Jain**
C.E.O., B. Jain Publishers (P) Ltd.

# CONTENTS

*Preface*   iii

*Acknowledgements*   v

*Publisher's Note*   vii

Introduction   1

1. Honey through the Centuries –   5
   In Different Cultures and in Religious Texts
2. Making of the Honey   13
3. The Composition of Honey   15
4. Types of Honey   17
5. Preserving Honey   79
6. Uses of Honey   81
7. Honey Recipes   85
8. As a Cosmetic   99
9. As a Medicine   107
10. Honey and Sports and Games   117
11. Mead   119
12. Honey-safety and Allergic Properties   121
13. Unusual Uses of Honey and Honey Bees   123
14. Trivia   125

## INTRODUCTION

Honey is a natural food filled with the goodness of nature. Manufactured by honey bees in their hives either in the wild or in controlled apiaries (a bee farm where beekeepers maintain hives for commercial production), it a well loved and accepted sweetener from the ancient times.

Just as there are six sides to the basic hexagonal structure in honeycombs, bees also provide humankind with six different useful products.

- Honey
- Pollen
- Royal jelly
- Propolis
- Beeswax
- Venom

## HONEY

Honey bees are generally associated with their main product honey. It is a sweet liquid whose colour generally ranges from almost white, to pale yellow, to amber and finally to a dark brown. Its texture also varies from a clear, free-flowing liquid to a thicker, darker, viscous solution. It is the healthiest and best sweetener known. It has nutritional value, medicinal value and cosmetic value.

## POLLEN

When bees collect nectar from flowers, pollen sticks to their legs. Honey bees facilitate pollination in plants and also use pollen as a source of their food and food for their larvae.

Bee pollen is nutritious and is used as a food supplement as well as an ingredient in the cosmetic industry. The composition of bee pollen depends on the type of flower from which the pollen is gathered.

It is a documented fact that some people are allergic to bee pollen and pollen can trigger a wide range of allergies and some may even go into anaphylactic reactions after consuming small amounts of it. Sensitive individuals should use bee pollen judiciously and carefully, if they have an inherent sensitivity to pollen. It may be better if such individuals totally avoid bee pollen.

## ROYAL JELLY

Worker bees secrete a substance called royal jelly. This substance is used as food for larvae and the queen bee.

Royal jelly is a highly perishable substance collected from the queen cells and is sold as a dietary supplement. It is a nutritious substance. Many healing powers have been attributed to it though there isn't much recorded evidence of its extraordinary healing properties. There are some benefits but more research has to be done to substantiate this fact. However, it is nutritious and has simple sugars, small amounts of B Vitamins, fats and amino acids. It also contains trace amounts of minerals and enzymes all of which are good for general health.

Some people are allergic to royal jelly. Symptoms similar to asthma and other allergic reactions have been observed in sensitive individuals. Royal jelly is expensive. It is good for general health but still has not been proven to be a total cure for any disease. It is often available as capsules. It is advisable not to use this product if you think it may cause allergies in you.

## PROPOLIS

Propolis is obtained when honey bees collect a resin-like substance from various parts of the tree or plant mainly from buds and sap. This resinous substance is used to seal small gaps or open spaces in bee hives. Propolis varies in colour from white to black taking on hues of green and red as well. It is often dark brown. The colour depends on the type of trees from which the resin is collected. This natural resin is often collected from the buds of Conifer trees and/or Poplar trees.

Propolis finds extensive use in traditional, natural and alternative medicine. It has several commercial uses including its use as a varnish for the wood used in musical instruments, as a food supplement and as a medicine to cure various ailments and conditions.

## BEESWAX

Beeswax is a natural wax produced by honey bees as oval and irregular flakes from their bodies. The bees build the cells in their honeycomb with wax. The larvae and young bees are raised in these cells. The honeycomb cells also store the pollen collected by the bees and the honey manufactured by them.

Beeswax is a commercially relevant product. It has multiple uses. It is used to make fine candles as well as in cosmetic and pharmaceutical formulations. It may be used to smoothen the surface of musical instruments including the tambourine or even as part of furniture polish together with linseed oil or turpentine. It has historically been used in the firearm industry. It may be used to impart a floral taste to manufacture floral gums, jelly beans and a few varieties of chocolates. It is also used to make unique jewellery. Various art forms including paintings and models also utilise beeswax and it is even used to make crayons.

## VENOM

Honey bee venom is also known as apitoxin. Bee venom is collected in collection frames using a mild electric shock to stimulate the bees to deposit their venom on these frames. Modern collection methods do not kill bees. It is a bitter and colourless liquid containing a complex mixture of proteins. It may be used to treat a variety of conditions including relieving the pain caused by rheumatism, arthritis and other conditions. It has anticoagulant and anti-inflammatory properties.

Honey bee venom is available as a venom cream, as capsules or in combination with honey. It may cause allergies or anaphylaxis in some sensitive individuals.

# 1

# HONEY THROUGH THE CENTURIES

## IN DIFFERENT CULTURES AND IN RELIGIOUS TEXTS

Honey bees precede human beings in their existence by millions of years. They were a part of the planet much before humankind appeared on earth. Hence, it is difficult to put a date as to when humankind realised the goodness of honey and its various uses.

Ancient Sumerian and Babylonian civilisations have mentioned honey in their cuneiform dating back to 2100 BC. Sacred Egyptian and Indian texts also mention honey favourably. In fact, honey has been mentioned and exalted as an auspicious substance in many recorded findings across various cultures, religions and civilisations. It is truly a food 'of and from the gods'.

The earliest pictorial recorded finding to date is a rock painting in a cave near Valencia in Spain. This painting dating back to 6000 BC shows a human figure climbing up to a beehive to gather honey. Several other rock paintings depicting the gathering of honey have been found in various countries in Africa. Carbon dating has marked a fossil bee to have been present on the earth fifty million years ago. The human use and sometimes abuse of bees may have started around ten thousand years ago.

Religious texts and ancients writings including the Quran, the Bible, the Torah, the Vedas and ancient Chinese and Buddhist scripts speak eloquently of the virtues of honey as a natural food for humankind. It has received the highest praise as a beneficial food from all the major religious texts in the world. Virtually every culture and ancient and modern civilisation has spoken of or used honey through the ages. Attributing it with religious, magical and beneficial values has been the norm. Some of its beneficial value has been substantiated by researchers from all over the world. There are also various folk tales and poems in several languages and dialects including popular ones from Finland and Ireland endorsing the importance of honey.

All major religions exalt the virtues of honey, its products and the hardworking honey bees. The bees themselves have been attributed to possess many qualities such as harmony, prudence, selflessness, teamwork and productivity and they teach humankind the same. They are also said to possess certain virtues like bravery, strength, and wisdom which human beings also wish to acquire.

For a long time, honey was the only natural known sweetener and hence, it occupied a place of reverence in everyday life.

Many ancient and thriving civilisations have also recorded the use of honey from ages. They include:

- India
- China
- Egypt
- The Mesopotamian Civilization
- Greece
- Rome
- Medieval Europe
- Africa

- Central and South America
- The Middle East

## INDIA

Religious texts in India dating to around 1000 BC speak of honey. The Rig Veda mentions honey. The ancient medicine and healing systems in India mention honey very favourably and honey has been used in various medical formulations. Prehistoric rock paintings depicting honey bees have been found in many parts of India.

Many Indians consider honey to be a food of the gods. It is used to celebrate various important functions including marriage. It has also been used as a skin and health tonic for cosmetic purposes.

Indians have been gathering honey from the forests from a very long time. In fact, even today many tribes and individuals spend a lot of their time gathering natural honey from the wild. There are many apiaries present in India. However, most of the honey is still gathered from rural and tribal farmers and sold to large cooperatives for processing. Beekeeping is a popular vocation in many parts of the country. There are also a few indigenous plants and shrubs from which the bees gather nectar to make honey.

Forest honey is mainly multifloral. However, there are small producers who also manufacture unifloral honey in India.

## CHINA

Around the 6th century BC in China, the book of songs or Shi Jin mentions honey. The Chinese have used honey more as a medicine rather than as a sweetener. Honey bees have been considered sacred and have been part of Emperor's flags as well as have been carved on small stones including jade.

Honey has been used as gifts for important officials and friends. Honey also formed a part of the rations bestowed upon high ranking Chinese government officials.

## EGYPT

Ancient hieroglyphics in Egypt depict drawings showing honey and honey bees. They date to around 2400 BC and suggest that beekeeping had been practiced as a craft. Both honey and honey bees were considered to be sacred. Drawings of honey and honey bees have also been found on the walls of royal tombs along with jars holding honey and honey products.

Ancient Egyptians used honey not only for religious ceremonies but honey was also considered as a high prized sweetener and gift. It found use in celebrations including marriages. It even formed a part of the wages or rations of government officials with high ranks.

Ancient medical texts from Egypt, written on carefully preserved papyrus, explain the use of honey in healing ulcers, skin gashes, open wounds and as an antiseptic.

## THE MESOPOTAMIAN CIVILISATIONS

All the three ancient civilisations – the **Assyrian**, the **Sumerian** and the **Babylonian** – gave honey and honey bees a high position in their cultures. Honey and honey products including beeswax were used in the worship of their ancient gods for various rites and rituals and also as sacred offerings to the gods.

The Assyrians used honey based products to treat conditions related to the eyes and the ears. Honey was also used in embalming dead bodies.

## GREECE

Honey has been a part of Greek myth and folk lore. The ancient Greek God Dionysus is credited to be the first god who made the hives and collected honey from them. Honey is considered sacred and the Greeks even believed that honey came straight from heaven. The honey bee holds its pride of place in Ancient Greece. The honey bee is depicted as a sacred symbol. The Greeks also used honey to preserve dead bodies.

Famous Greek thinkers and philosophers including Pythagoras, Plato, Hesiod, Aristophanes and Varro praised and exalted honey to great heights. Aristotle and his disciple Aristoxenus believed in the curative properties of honey. Hippocrates extolled the virtues of honey. Dioscorides, an expert in Greek medicine wrote that honey was good to treat sunburns, spots on the face, inflammation of the tonsils and throat and to cure coughs.

Many Greeks used to and still believe that the best honey comes from Attica, an important region in ancient and modern day Greece.

## ROME

Classic writers including Pliny, Vergil and Varro favourably mention honey in their writings. Pliny the Elder said that honey together with aloe could cure abrasions, bruises and burns. He also said that honey cured throat ailments and paralysis as well as other problems including ear and head infections. Other medical writers like Galen believed that warm honey was good for ear infections and Marcellus Empiricus believed that honey in combination with butter and rose oil could treat ear pain and treat certain eye ailments. It is said that Julius Caesar accepted honey in lieu of taxes.

## MEDIEVAL EUROPE

Around 1000 BC Saxon herbalists have mentioned that honey may be used to treat all kinds of wounds, to treat amputated limbs and to remove scabs. Anonymous scripts belonging to the fifteenth century speak of using honey with alum to treat skin ulcers and by early seventeenth century many authors including German ones speak of the use of honey in treating coughs, colds, wounds and ulcers. By mid eighteenth century the first book about honey in English, was published. It detailed the importance of honey to treat coughs, colds, tuberculosis and hoarseness.

## AFRICA

Africa has a large number of wild honey bees. The origin of the honey bee has been pinpointed to Africa. The varied climate and ecology of the continent makes it a producer of various types of honey. Traditional healers, many of them from Nigeria, Ghana and Mali have used and still use honey extensively in their long established treatments.

In Africa, honey is used in a variety of ways and for several purposes. During weddings, Africans use honey in large quantities. Hence the price of honey increases in this season. Africans use honey as food, in drinks including a special drink called Tej (it is a local/national honey wine), as a medicine and for different rites and rituals that have an ancient cultural heritage.

The entire continent has been using honey, though production follows traditional rather than modern methods. Many producers are small scale and most of the honey produced is used for local consumption. Thus the tradition continues. Beeswax is also used but its potential still needs to be explored as there are not many modern manufacturing processes to extract its possible use.

## CENTRAL AND SOUTH AMERICA

Long before Columbus landed on the shores of the Americas, Central and South Americans have been using honey, as an offering 'to and from the gods'.

Ancient Mexicans used honey more as a medicine rather than as a sweetener. Native Brazilians have used honey to treat a large number of ailments and conditions including bronchitis, colds, coughs, diabetes, impotence and sore throats.

## THE MIDDLE EAST

The Middle East has been the region where the three major religions of the world – Judaism, Christianity and Islam originated. All these three religions speak well of honey in their ancient texts. They also use honey in rites and rituals which are still followed to date.

While, the Middle East may not be a large producer of honey, the entire region is a large consumer of honey. Yemen is the largest producer of honey in the Middle East.

# 2

# MAKING OF THE HONEY

Honey is made from nectar naturally present in flowers. It can also be made from honeydew. Honey bees use their long tongues, just as we use straws, to draw out nectars from several flowers and accumulate this nectar in their special honey stomachs. (They have two stomachs – one is a honey storing stomach and the other is a regular stomach). They fill these honey stomachs by visiting anywhere between a hundred to fifteen hundred flowers. After filling their stomachs, they visit their beehives.

**Fig. 2.1** *Honey Bee*

In the beehives another set of bees, called the worker bees, suck the nectar out of the honey bees' stomach using their mouths. These worker bees or house bees 'chew' this nectar for around thirty minutes. This is the time when the nectar consisting of complex substances, including sugars, is broken down to form simple sugars mainly glucose and fructose. These simple sugars are easy to digest and have a longer shelf life when stored in the hives.

The nectar now consisting mainly of simple sugars and moisture is spread throughout the honeycombs. The process of

Fig. 2.2 *Bee Hive*

evaporation of moisture begins in these honeycombs. The bees also help in evaporating moisture faster by fanning the honeycombs with their wings. The honey remains in the honeycombs and is cured and thickens as it matures. When the honeycombs are filled with honey, the excess moisture evaporates so that it reaches an optimal moisture content. When the honey is thick enough as per the bees' specifications (generally less than 20 percent moisture content) the bees close or cap these cells with a special wax called beeswax to preserve the fresh honey to be used as their food. After the sealing process, the honey continues to mature and ripen in the honeycomb as a result of the enzymes present in the honey.

The honey is then stored in the honeycombs and is used by the bees as per their requirement. In commercial production, the honey is removed by the apiarists and sold as raw honey or is processed and sold as different grades of honey, the grades depending on various factors.

Plant sucking insects mainly aphids secrete honeydew. Insects from the order of insects called Hemiptera stab the foliage or other parts of certain plants and feed on the plant sap. This sap goes through the insects' gut and the excess is excreted as honeydew droplets. Bees gather these droplets and the honey is called honeydew honey.

Some people refer to honey as liquid gold and it is indeed so, as certain varieties of honey have a honey gold appearance. Honey is a sweet, nutritious substance health wise and taste wise; and is considered by some to be worth its weight in gold.

# 3
# THE COMPOSITION OF HONEY

Honey is composed of many wonderful substances, all of which are good for health. Floral honey consists mainly of moisture (water) and simple sugars such as glucose and fructose. These are the major components present in honey. It also contains small quantities of compound sugars including sucrose and maltose. It has trace elements such as enzymes, vitamins, minerals and amino acids. It also contains antioxidants.

When compared with floral honey, honeydew generally contains more complex sugars. Honeydew also contains trace amounts of amino acids and vitamins and minerals. It is generally seen that the darker the honey, the more the amount of trace minerals present.

As with other foods, there are some people who adulterate natural foods, decreasing their nutritional content. Sugarcane juice or corn syrup (generally much cheaper in cost than honey) may be added as natural adulterants. By analysing its composition, it is possible to check the authenticity of the honey. Floral honey contains many aromatic compounds and phenols which may be difficult to test but are markers that authenticate the naturalness of honey.

# TYPES OF HONEY

What are the types of honey? The answer to this question may depend on the country you are buying the honey in or the country where the honey has been manufactured or even blended. Different countries classify honey as per their standards.

Common classification of honey may be done in two ways:
1. Floral sources
2. Processing and packaging methods

## FLORAL SOURCES

There are hundreds of different floral sources of honey. Bees may gather nectar or honeydew from floral sources to make these different types of honey. Floral honey is sometimes also called blossom honey or nectar honey.

- Blended Honey
- Monofloral Honey
- Polyfloral Honey
- Honeydew Honey

### 1. BLENDED HONEY

Blended honey as the name suggests is a blend of various honeys procured from several floral sources. Commercially produced honey is generally blended honey. The different honeys may be from a single or several geographical locations and have varying physical and chemical characteristics.

Honey procured from various sources is blended together in large holding tanks. The resulting homogeneous mixture is then packaged. Blending honey together tends to create a consistent colour and flavour. It is thus easier to market these standardized honeys at retail outlets. Blended honey may also be more in demand as it may have judicious combinations of honey obtained from various sources. Conversely, it may not always be as suitable to the palate as monofloral honey, since an individual may get used to a certain honey taste that is a desired characteristic of monofloral honeys.

## 2. MONOFLORAL HONEY

As the name suggests monofloral honey is honey obtained when bees draw nectar from a single species of plant or tree. It is also called unifloral honey or single source honey. It is not possible to get 100% nectar from a single source. However, beekeepers ensure plantations of a single species over a large area or ensure that there is a blooming season of a particular plant to ensure harvesting of monofloral honeys. They may also position beehives to ensure that nectar is withdrawn from blossoms of particular plants. These honeys are relatively pure and have their own distinctive taste, colour and flavour. Within the same species of plant, there may be distinctions in taste of monofloral honey as the same species of honey obtained from different geographical locations may have seen different weather patterns in a particular year or a different "blooming" season. This may have some effect on the physical characteristics of the honey.

Monofloral honey is generally more expensive than polyfloral honey. Its taste may vary though there are always distinctive undertones of the floral source of nectar. The colour and texture generally varies from clear to coloured and from smooth to creamy. Since it is an expensive product, there is a high scope for adulteration. There are various methods used including chromatography to assess the monofloral source of honeys. Various parameters and calculating statistical parameters can be used to authenticate monofloral honey.

It is said that there are over 300 varieties of honey. There are many native honeys which may or may not be known outside their geographical location. However, there is a flourishing trade in a large number of monofloral honeys worldwide. There are a wide variety of single species that are used by apiarists to produce these specific honeys. Some of them are:

- Acacia Honey
- Alfalfa Honey
- Almond tree Honey
- Apple blossom Honey
- Avocado Honey
- Basswood/Lime/Linden Honey
- Blueberry Honey
- Buckwheat Honey
- Cherry blossom Honey
- Chestnut Honey
- Clover Honey
- Cotton Honey
- Eucalyptus Honey
- Fireweed Honey

- Gallberry Honey
- Goldenrod Honey
- Hawthorn Honey
- Heather Honey
- Jarrah Honey
- Jujube or Yemen Sidr Honey
- Kamahi Honey
- Kiawe Honey
- Lavender Honey
- Leatherwood Honey
- Lehua Honey
- Lemon tree Honey
- Litchi Honey
- Macadamia Honey
- Manuka Honey
- Mesquite Honey
- Mustard Honey
- Neem Honey
- Nodding thistle Honey
- Orange blossom Honey
- Pohutukawa Honey
- Pumpkin Blossom Honey
- Raspberry Honey
- Rata Honey
- Rewarewa Honey
- Rosemary Honey
- Sage Honey

## Types of Honey

- Saguaro Honey
- Sourwood Honey
- Star thistle Honey
- Strawberry Honey
- Sunflower Honey
- Tawari Honey
- Tulip tree or Poplar Honey
- Tupelo Honey
- Ulmo Honey
- Viper's Bugloss Honey
- Wild thyme Honey

## ACACIA HONEY

**Fig. 4.1** *Acacia Honey*

Acacia may be either a tree or a shrub. Since there are a variety of shrubs and trees, Acacia are found in many parts of the world. They are found most often in Tasmania, Australia, Argentina, Central America, North America, Europe and Africa. Some species also grow in the wild in the West Indies, in the Sinai Desert and the Jordan Valley.

Honey bees forage among the Acacia flowers, draw nectar from them and produce a delicately flavoured honey with a light and mild flowery taste. The honey has a liquid texture and flows well. It is almost as clear in appearance as glass and does not crystallise easily.

Acacia honey is one of the most popular honeys in the world. Many consumers prefer this honey as it looks clear and has a colourless to pale golden colour. Children are generally fond of it. It has a nice flavour similar to that of vanilla. Since it does not crystallise easily, it stays liquid for long periods of time. It has a high fructose content and hence is sweeter than honeys with lower fructose content and it also tends to crystallise less when compared with other honeys.

## USES

While sweetening beverages it does not add any strong flavours and is thus popular as a sweetener in beverages including sports drinks and teas. It also makes a good accompaniment to fresh ricotta cheese. It is spread on toast and is sometimes used for baking and can be an ingredient in steamed puddings.

**Fig. 4.2** *Acacia Flowers*

It is also used as an ingredient in natural hair conditioners especially for coloured hair to enhance colour and to increase shine.

The Acacia plant has medicinal value and some research studies indicate that the honey may also have higher medicinal value when compared to other sources of honey.

## ALFALFA HONEY

Alfalfa is widely grown throughout the world. It is also called Lucerne. This flowering leguminous plant is found in abundance

Fig. 4.3 *Alfalfa Flower*

in America, Australia, Canada, the United Kingdom, South Asia, South Africa and New Zealand.

The pretty purple Alfalfa blossoms yield a honey that is light in colour and has a rich flavour and pleasant yet delicate flavour with slightly minty undertones. The honey crystallises easily.

## USES

Since it has a mild and yet pleasant flavour which is not overpowering, Alfalfa honey may be considered as one of the first monofloral honeys a novice to honey may begin experimenting with.

It is used as table honey and may also be used in baking.

## ALMOND TREE HONEY

Fig. 4.4 *Honey Being Collected*

The Almond tree is a deciduous tree that bears beautiful white to pink blossoms in spring and bees happily pollinate these trees as they are drawn to the nectar present in the flowers. The nectar has amygdalin, a substance that is toxic to mammals, but has no such effect on bees. Studies have shown that it is may be a factor that attracts the bees as potential pollinators. The bees pollinate the tree and also make delicious Almond honey.

The honey has a light and pleasant golden appearance. It has a mild yet sweet taste. It has a mild aftertaste of almonds and sometimes may have mild sour notes. It does not crystallise easily and when it does the crystals are fine and small ones.

## USES

Almond tree honey is used as table honey. It is also used as an ingredient in baking especially while making biscuits.

## APPLE BLOSSOM HONEY

Apples are grown in many parts of the world especially in cooler climes. When the Apple tree blooms, the entire tree is filled with beautiful pristine white blossoms that fill the neighbourhood with a mild scent of apple. So it is no wonder that Apple blossom honey has a mild aroma of apples.

**Fig. 4.5** *Apple Tree Honeycomb*

**Fig. 4.6** *Apple Blossom Flower*

Different varieties of apples may lead to a slight difference in the taste of the honey especially with reference to a mild tartness in flavour which may be characteristic of some apple varieties or its sweetness which may be characteristic of other species. Apple blossom honey is clear and light gold in colour.

## USES

It is mainly used to sweeten hot tea and is also drizzled on freshly cut fruit.

## AVOCADO HONEY

The Avocado grows in parts of North America, Central America, Australia and Mexico. It is a common crop in tropical regions. Cream coloured Avocado blossoms provide nectar for honey bees to manufacture Avocado honey.

Avocado honey is dark in colour. It has a rich taste with buttery overtones.

## USES

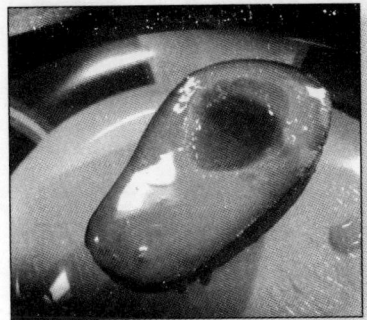

It may be used as a breakfast sweetener with cereals, oats or even on a slice of bread. It is used to glaze meat dishes and also for vinegar based salad dressings. It also adds a rich and unique flavour to a hot cup of coffee.

**Fig. 4.7** *Avocado Honey*

Avocado honey is often used as an ingredient for natural products including face cleansers and masks.

## BASSWOOD HONEY

The Basswood tree grows and flourishes all over North America. It is also known as the Linden tree or the Lime tree. It grows easily in Denmark. It is often planted in home gardens. Linden honey is produced not only in Denmark but is also quite popular in Slovenia, Romania, Poland and parts of Russia.

It is called Basswood honey or Linden honey in North America whereas it is sold as Lime honey in Europe and in the United Kingdom. This ornamental tree has fragrant blossoms whose nectar gives Basswood honey its pleasant aroma.

Basswood honey has a light yellow or golden appearance. It has a delicate and mild yet distinctive flavour with deep overtones. It has a pleasant and woody aroma and a floral aftertaste. It crystallises easily. The flavour of the honey lingers for a long time.

Fig. 4.8 *Basswood Flowers*

## USES

Fig. 4.9 *Basswood* Honey

Basswood honey is used to sweeten teas, to drizzle over green apples, as an accompaniment to mild white cheeses and with vanilla ice cream. It may also be used as a marinade and as a dressing for various salads.

It has a lot of medicinal value and is recommended for a wide variety of ailments including anxiety, insomnia, bronchitis, coughs and colds.

## BLUEBERRY HONEY

Bees draw honey from the white flowers of the Blueberry plant and produce a honey that is light amber in colour. It has a pleasant flavour with an aftertaste of Blueberries. It may granulate over a period of time.

**Fig. 4.10** *Blueberry* Flowers

**Fig. 4.11** *Blueberries*

## USES

**Fig. 4.12** *Blueberry Honey*

Blueberry honey is mainly used as a table honey. It may be used to flavour yogurts and in making jams. It can also be spread on muffins, toast and pancakes. It may be used as a sweetener in teas. It is also used in cosmetic products like softeners and face washes.

## BUCKWHEAT HONEY

Bees gather nectar from the tiny and fragrant pink flowers of the Buckwheat plant which grows in many parts of the world. It is found abundantly in America, Canada, Siberia, Eastern Europe, northern parts of India, Japan, China, Russia, Poland, Brazil, South Africa and Manchuria.

**Fig. 4.13** *Buckwheat Flowers*

**Fig. 4.14** *Buckwheat Plant*

It is a dark honey. It has a pleasant and hay like earthy aroma. It has a strong and almost spicy flavour which lingers on. It resembles molasses both in its colour and its viscosity.

Since it has a dark appearance and a strong flavour, Buckwheat honey is the preferred choice of honey while making mead. Dark honeys are also richer in antioxidants and thus have more medicinal value.

## USES

The medicinal benefits of Buckwheat honey has been researched for curing coughs and for alleviating various symptoms in various diseases and even in studies conducted on methods to prevent premature ageing. Buckwheat honey is often used to cure coughs and is especially given to children as an alternative to OTC (Over the Counter) cough syrups.

It is used as a drizzle over pancakes, to make honey based cakes and in poultry, beef and pork dishes. It is used in sauces and as a drizzle over ice cream. It may be paired with strong cheeses.

Fig. 4.15 *Dark Buckwheat Honey*

## CHERRY BLOSSOM HONEY

Fig. 4.16 *Cherry Blossom Flowers*

Cherry blossom being the national flower of Japan, there is no doubt that this honey is popular in Japan. Though not as easily available as many other monofloral honeys it is also popular in the United Kingdom. The Cherry tree grows in many other countries including France, Greece, Rome and China but more than its honey, its fruits i.e. cherries are of economic importance.

Cherry Blossom honey is light coloured with a slightly fruity taste and may have a mild aroma reminiscent of cherries. It is a gourmet honey. Although in demand, it is not easily available as other monofloral honeys, not even in the United Kingdom or in Japan.

## USES

It is used as a table honey and to flavour ice creams.

**Fig. 4.17** *Cherry Blossom Honey*

## CHESTNUT HONEY

**Fig. 4.18** *Chestnut Honey*

The Chestnut tree grows in many parts of the world. It is popular in Italy, Switzerland, Spain, China, Turkey, South Korea and France.

All dark honeys are rich in antioxidants and Chestnut honey, which is a dark honey, also has a high mineral content when compared with other honeys.

This honey has a light to dark amber colour and is quite a strong honey. It has a distinctive taste. It is intense, with some pungency and a mild aftertaste of sourness or bitterness mainly due to its acidic components. Generally, this honey has a distinctive woody aroma and earthy taste.

**Fig. 4.19** *Honey in Cakes*

It does not crystallise easily and stays liquid for long periods of time.

## USES

Chestnut honey is a good accompaniment for several cheeses especially seasoned ones. It is also used as a sweetener for several desserts including ice creams, cakes, tarts and while baking fruits especially pears. It is also drizzled over meats or used as a glaze or as a sauce when cooking different meats.

## CLOVER HONEY

Clover grows in the United States, Canada, New Zealand, Ireland and parts of Europe including Holland.

Clover honey is a clear honey with a white to almost yellow coloured appearance or is light amber. As there are a wide variety of Clover blossoms including Red Clover, Alsike Clover, White and Yellow Sweet Clover, the colour depends on the type of Clover from which the honey bee draws its nectar.

When nectar from White Clover blossoms is made into honey by the bees, it has a very clear appearance and light colour that it is even called white honey by some as it may have a silvery white appearance.

It is a light and subtle honey. It has a delicate flavour and mild sweetness with floral overtones.

## USES

It is mainly used as a table honey, in sauces, salad dressings and for some baked goods.

**Fig. 4.20** *Honey on the Table*

## COTTON HONEY

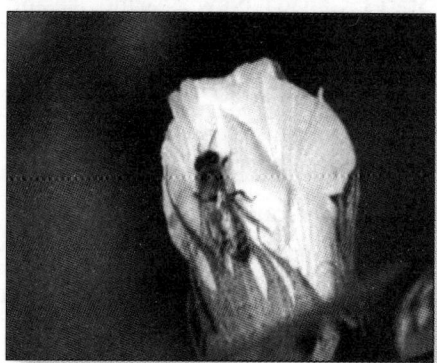

**Fig. 4.21** *Cotton Flower*

Cotton honey may be considered as a predominantly Asian honey as cotton survives and flourishes in many parts of Asia especially Central and South Asia including India. It also grows in abundance in many parts of the world including the United States.

Cotton honey has a light amber appearance. It has a creamy texture. It has a mild and pleasant almost buttery flavour and a low acidity. It crystallises quite rapidly.

Compared to other monofloral honeys, Cotton honey is more easily available. It may be used both as a table honey and may be spread on biscuits, toast or pancakes. It is also used to make various desserts including cakes and pastries.

## EUCALYPTUS HONEY

Native to Australia, the Eucalyptus tree has spread its medicinal value worldwide after its cultivation had begun in India, Africa, Europe and the United States. There are a wide variety of Eucalyptus species, over five hundred of them, growing in most parts of the world. There are different types of flowers whose colours range from white to pink.

The colour of Eucalyptus honey is generally dark amber. It

**Fig. 4.22** *Eucalyptus Flowers*

has a strong and intense flavour which lingers on as an aftertaste. It has overtones of menthol. There may be a difference in the taste of the honey as it is difficult to specify the variety of eucalyptus from which the honey has been obtained. It crystallises easily. It is quite expensive. It is manufactured to a great extent in Australia, Africa and India.

**Fig. 4.23** *Honey as an Intense Flavour*

## USES

Eucalyptus honey is used for sweetening beverages including tea, in making pastries and as an accompaniment for cheeses. It is also used for its medicinal properties to heal wounds, aches and pains and throat infections and for beauty products formulated especially for the skin.

## FIREWEED HONEY

**Fig. 4.24** *Fireweed Flower*

Fireweed grows in parts of Canada and the United States from Alaska to California. Fireweed grows naturally amidst forests that have been ravaged due to wild forest fires. Fireweeds are wildflowers that begin the natural renewal process in forests. The flowers bloom for just over a week. Nectar is extracted from attractive purplish pink Fireweed flowers.

This honey is light amber in colour and has an enviable clarity which distinguishes it from other darker honeys. It has a delicate taste with buttery overtones. It has a smooth texture. It is considered to be a premium honey and is revered by one and all as it is quite difficult to obtain and when obtained, the quantities are small.

Fireweed honey is used for baking, grilling, smoking foods and as a glaze especially for gourmet foods.

## GALLBERRY HONEY

Gallberry honey is obtained from small evergreen holly bushes. The bush is also called Inkberry or Evergreen Winterberry. Tiny white flowers filled with nectar blossom every spring and thus honey bees sip this nectar to manufacture an amber coloured honey.

**Fig. 4.25** *Gallberry Flower*

This honey is produced in certain parts of the United States. It has a white to amber appearance and a rich yet subtle taste. It does not crystallise easily.

## USES

**Fig. 4.26** *Gallberry Honey*

Gallberry honey is a thick honey that is used mainly as a table honey. It may also be used while baking goods, as a substitute for sugar or corn syrup or it may be drizzled over boiled or baked carrots, fried chicken or as a topping on vanilla ice cream.

## GOLDENROD HONEY

Fig. 4.27 *Goldenrod Flower*

One of the last flowers, blossoming in late summer just before autumn sets in, honey bees collect nectar from bright yellow Goldenrod blossoms and convert it to honey. Goldenrod honey is a distinctive monofloral honey.

It has a light to medium amber colour and a strong and distinct aroma. It has a thick texture and a unique taste. It granulates quite easily.

## USES

Despite its strong odour and taste some people use it to sweeten tea. It is used as an ingredient in bakery products. When making Mead, many brewers prefer using Goldenrod honey.

Fig. 4.28 *Golden rod Honey*

## HAWTHORN HONEY

Fig. 4.29 *Hawthorn Flower*

The Hawthorn is often grown as a hedge plant in most parts of England, Ireland and Scotland. It is also known as the May Bush or Whitethorn. It thrives in meadows, beside brooks and also in open woods. It also grows in Europe, Asia and Africa. It has been naturalized in other parts of the world including the United States.

Hawthorn honey is popular in the United Kingdom. It has a mildly bitter taste. it has been used both in folk and native medicines to cure certain ailments including cardiac conditions, hypertension and insomnia.

## USES

It may be used to sweeten tea. It has a dark brownish appearance. It is a full bodied honey with a rich and nutty flavour. It has a distinct aroma.

Fig. 4.30 *Thick-rich Honey*

## HEATHER HONEY

Fig. 4.31 *Heather in Scotland*

Generally, a modest little purple flower, the Heather blooms along the mountains in Scotland and in many parts of Europe including Germany. It has been widely introduced in New Zealand. White flowers of Heather which are rare blossoms are considered to be a symbol of good luck like the four leaf clover.

This honey is popular in the United Kingdom. This typical British honey is a highly prized food and has its fair share of lovers and haters who either love or hate its unique taste.

Heather honey is dark amber or brown in colour. It has a thick consistency. It has a fragrant and floral taste with mild pungency and a slightly bitter aftertaste. It has a strong aroma and does not granulate easily.

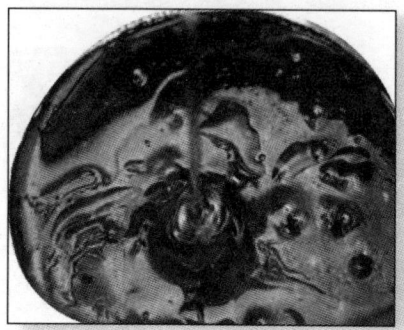

Fig. 4.32 *Dark Amber Heather Honey*

## USES

It is used to sweeten black coffee. It is used to prepare various meats, seafood and cold cuts. It is also used as a sweetener when making cakes or as a topping on cereal.

## JARRAH HONEY

This is a type of Eucalyptus honey native to Western Australia. It is a tall tree that may grow up to a height of 40 metres. It blooms during late spring and early summers when the trees are covered with beautiful cream coloured flowers. Honey bees collect nectar from these flowers to produce Jarrah honey.

Fig. 4.33 *Jarrah Flower*

The honey has a medium to dark amber appearance. It has a fairly unique taste with an aftertaste of caramel. It has a smooth texture. It is not very sweet when compared to some other honeys and also has a lower glycemic index. It does not crystallise easily.

## USES

Jarrah honey is used as a table honey. It has been attributed with medicinal properties and some research studies corroborate its antimicrobial efficacy. It is used to cure a wide range of ailments including coughs, sore throats, bad breath and to heal wounds.

**Fig. 4.34** *Jarrah Honey*

## JUJUBE OR YEMEN SIDR HONEY

**Fig. 4.35** *Yemen Sidr Flower*

The best Jujube honey is obtained from Yemen where these trees flourish in the wild The Jujube tree also grows in parts of the Arabian Peninsula, India, parts of Africa including Libya, Egypt, Ethiopia, Sudan and in Pakistan. The tree has many names including Jujube, Sidr, Lote Tree, Christ's thorn or Nabkh Tree. It is an ancient and sacred tree. Many parts of the tree have medicinal value. Bees forage among the Jujube flowers and produce an unparalleled honey according to some.

The honey has an appearance which may range from yellow to brown.

## USES

It has a unique taste. Research studies have indicated that Jujube honey has a high medicinal value. It is an expensive honey. It may be used as a table honey.

Fig. 4.36 *Yemen Sidr Honey*

## KAMAHI HONEY

Fig. 4.37 *Kamahi Flower*

This honey is obtained from the Kamahi trees that are native to New Zealand. The evergreen Kamahi tree flourishes mainly in the South Island of New Zealand. The flowers are white to cream in colour, bloom in spring and easily attract bees.

Kamahi honey is amber coloured ranging from light to mid amber. It has a strong taste with complex overtones but is sweet and hence it is not an overpowering honey. It crystallises quite easily. It is considered to be a premium honey.

## USES

It may be used when cooking vegetables and also in meat based dishes and in baked foods. It is sometimes used to sweeten teas.

Fig. 4.38 *Kamahi Honey*

## KIAWE HONEY

Kiawe trees grow in the arid volcanic environment that is characteristic of certain parts of Hawaii. Native to Hawaii these mesquite trees also grow in some of the other Pacific Islands.

Fig. 4.39 *Kiawe Flower*

It has a clear almost whitish appearance. It has a lovely taste and texture. It may crystallise easily.

Kiawe honey is almost always available as organic honey. It is a premium honey that competes for the category of best honey in the world among honey lovers but there is no clear verdict as many monofloral honeys have their own fan clubs among honey connoisseurs.

## USES

It may be used as a table honey.

Fig. 4.40 *Kiawe Honey*

## LAVENDER HONEY

Lavender is widely grown in many parts of the world- in Asia, in Africa, in Tasmania and even in parts of North America. It flourishes in Europe, especially in Spain, France, England and the Mediterranean. With its mauve to violet flowers, lavender attracts humans and

Fig. 4.41 *Lavender Flower*

bees alike. However, though we humans exult in the pleasant fragrance of Lavender, the bees also draw nectar from the flowers and produce a delicate honey-Lavender honey.

Pure Lavender honey has a pale appearance. It has a mid to light brown appearance. It has a delicate aroma and a delicious flavour. It crystallises quite easily.

## USES

Lavender honey is used to sweeten and flavour herbal teas. It is used to make cakes, in ice cream and in some other desserts. It is paired with a wide variety of cheeses especially soft cheeses and blue cheese. It is also used as an ingredient in face cleansers, hand balms and other beauty products.

**Fig. 4.42** *Lavender Honey*

## LEATHERWOOD HONEY

**Fig. 4.43** *Leatherwood Flower*

The Leatherwood grows profusely in the cool temperate climate of Tasmania and Australia. When it blossoms in late spring and early summer, the white flowers attract bees that forage and produce a unique honey, which may almost always have organic certification.

It is a honey that has gourmet value and is considered to be a delicacy by honey lovers. It has a distinctive taste. With a strong floral taste and a spicy flavour, it is a smooth and creamy iconic monofloral honey from Tasmania.

## USES

Leatherwood honey is used as a spread on toast (preferably whole wheat), to sweeten and flavour breakfast cereals and tea and as a sweetener to give not only taste but also a fragrant aroma to cakes and muffins. It is also popular as a drink in combination with fresh lemon juice.

## LEHUA HONEY

**Fig. 4.44** *Lehua Flower*

The Ohi'a tree is a native hardwood tree that grows 4000 feet high on the northern side of the Mauna Kea volcano in Hawaii. It is considered to be a medicinal tree. Fragrant red Lehua flowers blossom and attract bees that gather around to collect nectar from these flowers and produce one of the rarest organic honeys in the world.

It is a monofloral honey obtained from the island of Hawaii. It is a premium honey and is very much in demand as it is a rare type of honey.

Lehua honey has a light toffee colour and has a smooth texture and slightly buttery taste. It has an aromatic fragrance. When freshly harvested it is generally liquid but may become creamy and more robust within a few weeks.

## USES

It is used to sweeten tea, may be applied thickly on freshly baked bread or on muffins or drizzled over freshly cut fruit or gourmet ice creams.

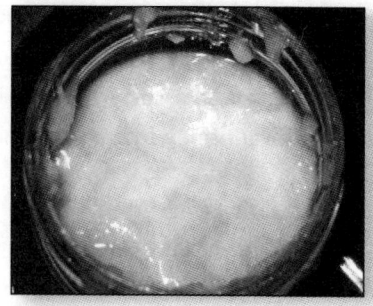

**Fig. 4.45** *Lehua Honey*

## LEMON TREE HONEY

**Fig. 4.46** *Lemon tree Flower*

The Lemon tree is a small evergreen tree. When it blossoms, white flowers edged with pink or purple colour cover the trees and attract bees in large numbers. The honey that is produced from these blossoms has a decidedly citrus flavour.

It is a clear honey with a pleasant citrusy aroma. It is often pale and light yellow in appearance. It has a fresh and intense flavour. It forms fine crystals and does not crystallise quickly. It has a sweet taste with mildly acidic overtones.

Studies conducted in Spain show that Lemon Blossom honey is pastier and coarser than Orange Blossom honey. It is also lumpier and less transparent when compared with other citrus honeys. It is quite popular in Mediterranean countries.

## USES

Lemon tree honey is used mainly to sweeten herbal teas. It is a good accompaniment to various cheeses. It may be used as an ingredient in vinaigrettes or to flavour different types of meats. It is said to have a mild sedative effect.

Fig. 4.47 *Lemon Tree Honey*

## LITCHI OR LYCHEE HONEY

Fig. 4.48 *Litchi Flower*

The Litchi flourishes in parts of North India especially in Bihar and Jharkhand. It is also grows in Thailand, Malaysia, Vietnam, South Africa and parts of the United States. The honey produced from the Litchi flowers is a premium honey. It is not easily available.

It has a light amber appearance. It is a thin honey with a pleasant aroma. It has a tangy and delicious taste with sweet and sour overtones.

## USES

Litchi honey may be used as a table honey. It is also used to sweeten tea. It may be drizzled over fresh fruits and ice cream.

Fig. 4.49 *Litchi Honey*

## MACADAMIA HONEY

The Macadamia tree grows in Australia, Hawaii, the United States and other countries in the world. This evergreen ornamental tree is valued for its products including Macadamia nuts and Macadamia oil.

**Fig. 4.50** *Macadamia Flower*

Macadamia honey has a light amber or sometimes deep amber colour. It combines sweetness and a nutty taste with a distinctively complex aroma.

## USES

**Fig. 4.51** *Macadamia Honey*

Macadamia honey is used as an ingredient in a wide variety of dishes including fruit and vegetable salads, as a marinade and also to caramelise poultry, red meat and a few vegetables for barbequing. It is also used as a topping on toast and on pancakes, to sweeten herbal teas, as a sweetener in ice cream and as a glaze for poultry dishes. It may be used to make biscuits, pastries, cakes, candies, nougat and pies.

## MANUKA HONEY

Manuka honey is obtained from the Tea tree or Manuka bush mainly in New Zealand. The flowers are generally white and at times pink in colour and attract bees in profusion.

**Fig. 4.52** *Manuka Flower*

Manuka honey may be graded with an UMF or Unique Manuka Factor, a rating that measures the non hydrogen peroxide antibacterial strength of the honey. Another way of grading the honey is to use a factor called the Molan Gold Standard.

Extensive research has been carried out on this honey. It is used as a medicine to treat coughs, colds, ulcers, indigestion and acne. Honeys with higher UMF have higher anti bacterial properties.

The honey has a dark amber appearance. It has an intense and distinctive almost mildly medicinal taste.

## USES

Most often it is used as a table honey. It is also used to sweeten beverages and may be used as an ingredient in medicines including wound dressings, in cooking and in cosmetics.

**Fig. 4.53** *Manuka Honey*

## MESQUITE HONEY

The Mesquite flourishes in parts of the United States, mainly in Arizona, Texas and in Mexico. It was later introduced to other continents including Asia, Africa and Australia. It has creamy white to light yellow flowers that attract honey bees.

Fig. 4.54 *Mesquite Flower*

This honey is obtained mainly from the Southwestern parts of Australia. It is dark brown in colour and has a viscous texture. It generally remains semi crystalline. It has a distinct flavour.

### USES

Fig. 4.55 *Mesquite Honey*

It has a sweet yet smoky aroma making it a popular glaze for barbequed meat. It may also be used as a table honey.

## MUSTARD HONEY

Both Black Mustard and the less common varieties of Yellow and Orange Mustard attract a lot of honey bees who suck in the nectar from its flowers to manufacture Mustard honey.

Fig. 4.56 *Mustard Flower*

The honey has a sweet flavour with mildly spicy overtones. It is manufactured in India and is popular in Germany and in the countries of the Middle East.

Although it may be difficult to obtain pure monofloral mustard honey a combination of honey and mustard seeds called mustard honey, which is actually a flavoured honey, is easily available. Sometimes these flavoured honeys may have other ingredients including pepper and spices.

## USES

It may be used as a table honey. However, as the name suggests, flavoured Mustard honey is used as an ingredient especially in savoury dishes.

**Fig. 4.57** *Mustard Honey*

## NEEM HONEY

**Fig. 4.58** *Neem Flower*

Considered auspicious in India, the Neem tree grows and flourishes all over India. It also grows in Myanmar and has been introduced to Africa, Australia, South America and the Middle East. Almost all its parts have medicinal value. In India, Neem honey has been used to treat various ailments. The small and attractive white flowers, which emit a sweet fragrance, attract bees who suck its nectar and produce honey.

Neem honey is dark amber in appearance. It has a strong and bitter taste.

## USES

Neem honey is used more as a medicine rather than as a sweetener. It is often used in Ayurvedic formulations. It is a much sought after honey. It is also used in cosmetic formulations including soaps, creams, cleansers and hand washes.

**Fig. 4.59** *Neem Honey*

## NODDING THISTLE HONEY

**Fig. 4.60** *Nodding Thistle Flower*

Also called Musk thistle, the Nodding Thistle is a weed species thriving in almost all parts of the world. Nodding Thistle blooms in late summer and produces brilliant mauve coloured flowers that attract bees. The Nodding Thistle may be considered a pesky weed by farmers and agriculturists but beekeepers treasure it as it provides a delectable and much sought after honey. Unfortunately it is still considered as a weed and as its proliferation is being checked, this honey is now obtained less easily when compared to earlier times. Nodding Thistle honey is obtained worldwide.

It has a light amber colour and is quite a well liked honey. It has a pleasant taste and floral aroma. It crystallises slowly.

## USES

It can be used to flavour a large number of dishes but its mild flavour makes it perfect for vegetable based dishes. It may also be used as a table honey and to sweeten teas.

## ORANGE BLOSSOM HONEY

**Fig. 4.61** *Orange Blossom Flower*

Native to Asia, the Orange tree spread to various countries in Europe including France and Spain. It is grown in many states of America including California, Florida and in Mexico. Small white flowers cover the tree and attract bees that pollinate the tree and produce a tasty honey from the nectar present in its flowers.

The honey obtained from Orange Blossoms is generally fragrant with a hint of the aroma of the Orange Blossoms. It is clear in appearance and generally has a light amber colour. According to some it has a pleasant flavour with a lingering taste of the orange itself. Others consider it to have a more citrusy or floral flavour. It has a strong aroma. It is a high quality and popular honey.

## USES

Orange Blossom honey is generally used as a table honey. It is also used to replace sugar in many baked goods especially in baked sweets, Madeleines, biscuits and granola. It is also used as a spread on bread, biscuits and pancakes. It may be used to sweeten both hot and cold teas. It is sometimes used to glaze meats and vegetables.

Fig. 4.62 *Orange Blossom Honey*

## POHUTUKAWA HONEY

Fig. 4.63 *Pohutukawa Flower*

Native to coastal New Zealand, the Pohutukawa tree is also known as the New Zealand Christmas tree. When the flowers blossom in December, honey bees are attracted to its brilliant crimson colour. Bees use the nectar to produce a delectable and very rare to obtain honey since the flowering season may sometimes be inconsistent.

Pohutukawa honey is white to pale gold in appearance. It has a sweet taste with a hint of floral overtones and a mildly salty tang as the tree grows in volcanic soil.

## USES

It is used as cooking honey for making different sauces. It is used as an ingredient when making lamb dishes. It is also used to bake cakes and to top ice cream or sweeten hot and cold beverages. It may be paired with certain cheeses including Pecorino, Gruyere and Emmental. It is also used to make skin care products including lip balms.

Fig. 4.64 *Pohutukawa Honey*

## PUMPKIN BLOSSOM HONEY

Fig. 4.65 *Pumpkin Blossom Flower*

The Pumpkin grows almost everywhere in the world, but when it blossoms, the flowers have a short life and it is essential that bees pollinate them at the earliest. In fact the reason why this honey is not easily available is that bees have to draw nectar within a short time from these blooming flowers as these short term flowers just fall from the pumpkin patch. The yellow male and female flowers generally open for only one day.

Pumpkin blossom honey is quite sweet with a mild yet spicy taste. It may have a hint of pumpkin in its flavour. It is a dark amber coloured honey. It has a floral fragrance. It is seasonal. As it is obtained in limited amounts and also has a pleasant taste it is considered as a gourmet honey.

## USES

It is used to make bread, in sweet and savoury sauces, as a topping, as a drizzle and as an ingredient for several desserts. It is used as a glaze with several different types of meats. It improves the taste of cakes, muffins, pies and tarts. It may be combined with butter and used to top bread, bagels, toast and scones. It is also a delicious topping on ice cream.

**Fig. 4.66** *Pumpkin Blossom Honey*

## RASPBERRY HONEY

**Fig. 4.67** *Raspberry Flower*

Raspberry is grown as a commercial crop worldwide and though it is a gourmet honey, Raspberry honey can be purchased from many countries. In early May, the white flowers blossom and bees descend on these attractive flowers to gather nectar and make a delicious Raspberry honey.

Raspberry honey is light to golden yellow in colour. It has a mild and yet sweet taste with the hint of a tart raspberry aftertaste which distinguishes it from other light honeys. It crystallises easily. Thus it is often made into a creamed honey. However it reverts to its liquid form when heated gently.

## USES

Raspberry honey is generally used as a table honey. It may

**Fig. 4.68** *Raspberry Honey*

be used to sweeten tea or is drizzled over toast and muffins. It is also paired with various fruits including peaches, pears and a few fresh cheeses or to top ice creams or flavour yogurts.

## RATA HONEY

Fig. 4.69 *Rata Flower*

It is obtained mainly from New Zealand. Although there are eight species of Rata, most of the honey is got from the nectar of the Southern Rata. The Rata also grows in the parts of Southeast Asia and also in the Pacific. With prolific red flowers in some seasons and erratic flowering in others Rata honey may or may not be produced in large quantities every year.

Pure Rata honey looks almost white in appearance. It is one of the lightest coloured honeys. It is not too sweet and has a distinct yet subtle flavour with a slightly salty aftertaste. It crystallises easily and is therefore popular as a creamed honey.

## USES

It is spread on toast or used as an ice cream topping. It is also used to produce honey based cosmetics.

Fig. 4.70 *Rata Honey*

## REWAREWA HONEY

**Fig. 4.71** *Rewarewa Flower*

The Rewarewa tree grows in mainly New Zealand, Australia and South Africa. It is obtained from the bright red Rewarewa flowers, flowers that have a needle like appearance.

It is a premium honey. It has a dark amber to brown appearance with a reddish tinge. It has a caramel like taste with a slightly buttery or burnt aftertaste. It is a smooth honey. It crystallises slowly. Rewarewa honey has high hydrogen peroxide activity.

## USES

It is used to flavour both sweet and spicy dishes, hot drinks and is also used as a spread. It may be used to sweeten teas and lemonade.

## ROSEMARY HONEY

The Rosemary is an ornamental plant as well as a popular herb. It may grow easily in many countries but it is native to and flourishes in the Mediterranean. It is obtained mainly from France and Spain.

Rosemary honey is a pale light coloured almost white

**Fig. 4.72** *Rosemary Flower*

honey. It has a mildly minty and woodsy flavour, with a subtle taste. It is a smooth honey.

## USES

Fig. 4.73 *Rosemary Honey*

This honey has many uses. It is used as a table honey and also to top ice creams. It is used in sauces and marinades with chicken, fish, lamb and vegetable dishes. It is also paired with different cheeses including goat cheeses and blue cheese. It is also used in cosmetics, mainly in hair conditioners.

## SAGE HONEY

This popular honey may be obtained when bees forage on flowers of three different varieties of sage including Black Button, Purple and White Sage. The Black Button begins its flowering season in February and though it continues till June, only one or two flowers bloom at a time among the various florets.

Fig. 4.74 *Sage Flower*

Sage honey is light in colour. It has a mild yet pleasant flavour with a slightly herbal aftertaste. It does not crystallise easily. It is not easy to obtain.

## USES

It may be used to sweeten teas. It is used as a glaze or sauce especially with game meats. It may be paired with different cheeses including parmesan. It may be drizzled over fruits, ice creams, biscuits and scones.

**Fig. 4.75** *Sage Honey*

## SAGUARO HONEY

**Fig. 4.76** *Saguaro Flower*

The Saguaro is a large cactus native to the Southwestern parts of America including Arizona, Mexico and California. The creamy white Saguaro blossoms attract bees which draw nectar to produce an interesting and popular honey. This desert wildflower is also the state flower of Arizona.

Saguaro honey is obtained from parts of the United States and Mexico. It is light or dark yellow in appearance. It crystallises quite easily. It is a rare honey and is not obtained easily. It is quite sweet with buttery overtones.

## USES

It is used as a table honey as well as in baking.

## SOURWOOD HONEY

Indigenous to the United States, the Sourwood tree grows mainly in Pennsylvania, Georgia and North Carolina. The blossoming

Fig. 4.77 *Sourwood Flower*

season, when white bell shaped flowers are present on its branches, is quite short and ranges from June to August.

Sourwood honey is a light coloured honey ranging from white to light amber and has a thin flowing texture. It has a sweet and delicate taste with a lingering floral taste with mild hints of fragrant spices like anise. It has a pleasant aroma. It does not crystallise easily. It is a rare and premium honey that is quite difficult to obtain.

## USES

It is a popular table honey. It is used to sweeten iced teas. It is used as an ingredient to make barbeque sauces and is a good honey to use when making Asian style sweet and sour dishes. It may also be spread on homemade butter biscuits to enhance their tasty flavour.

Fig. 4.78 *Sourwood Honey*

## STAR THISTLE

Native to the Mediterranean, the Star Thistle has flourished mainly in the United States. It is considered as a noxious weed by some but honey bees love its blossoms. It is a popular honey and is produced in most parts of America.

Fig. 4.79 *Star Thistle Flower*

It has a thick texture with a light to medium gold appearance. It is sweet with no lingering aftertaste and taste wise is considered by some as a milder and better version of Clover honey. It is often sold as a creamed honey.

## USES

Star Thistle honey is a table honey. It is a good drizzle on fruits and both hot and cold cereals and bagels. It is used to sweeten teas. It is also used in sauces, glazes, marinades and salad dressings. It is an accompaniment for various cheeses or cheese fondues. Some of the popular cheeses used include Brie, blue cheese, goat cheeses, ricotta and parmesan.

**Fig. 4.80** *Star Thistle Honey*

## STRAWBERRY HONEY

Cultivated all over the world, the Strawberry is a well loved fruit whose flavour is commercially extracted both as natural and synthetic derivatives.

This honey is quite rare and is not easily obtained. It has a fairly clear appearance. It is quite pungent and has a bitter taste that may not appeal to many honey gourmets. This may be the reason why it is difficult to obtain as monofloral honeys are not easily obtained.

**Fig. 4.81** *Strawberry Flower*

## USES

Fig. 4.82 *Strawberry Honey*

Strawberry honey is used as an accompaniment with cheeses including pecorino cheese. It has a tendency to crystallise.

## SUNFLOWER HONEY

As the Sunflower raises its head towards the sun, it not only forms a pretty picture and a sight to behold for us humans but it also attracts honey bees which draw nectar from it to produce a honey that has an appearance similar to the flower albeit a slightly lighter tint of yellow.

Fig. 4.83 *Sunflower*

It is commonly manufactured in various parts of the world. France, India, Italy, Spain and parts of the United States are among the leading producers.

Sunflower honey has a light yellow colour and pleasant appearance. It is a delicate and light honey. It has subtle floral undertones and a lovely aroma. It crystallises easily.

Fig. 4.84 *Sunflower Honey*

## USES

It is a table honey. it is used to sweeten teas and other hot drinks. It is often used as an ingredient to make biscuits, granola bars and is sometimes spread on toast.

## TAWARI HONEY

The Tawari tree is native and endemic to New Zealand and when it blooms it is a beautiful sight to behold. The Maoris, indigenous people of New Zealand, use its ornamental creamy white flowers to adorn themselves while the bees use the nectar present in these flowers to make a light honey with a memorable taste.

**Fig. 4.85** *Tawari Flowers*

It is a light honey with a pale appearance. It has a lovely golden hue. It has a subtle and mild flavour with undertones of butterscotch. It has a pleasant aroma.

## USES

Tawari honey is used to add flavour and sweetness to many desserts and baked goods including ice creams, pancakes and waffles. It is drizzled on fruits. It is also used to sweeten tea and lemon based beverages.

**Fig. 4.86** *Tawari Honey*

## TULIP TREE OR POPLAR HONEY

Poplar honey is obtained from Tulip trees mainly grown in the US and is an attractive tree native to Eastern United States. The tree is referred to as the Tulip tree, the Tulip Poplar, the Yellow Poplar, Whitewood, White Poplar, Canoe Wood or the American Tulip tree. It has been introduced and flourishes in parts of Europe. Tulip tree honey is a dark coloured honey with reddish hues.

**Fig. 4.87** *Tulip Flower*

## USES

Bakers and confectioners find this a good honey to use, when making confectionery. When compared with dark honeys that are generally strong in flavour, it has a mild flavour. As a table honey, it gets mixed reviews from consumers This honey is sometimes referred to as Poplar honey.

**Fig. 4.88** *Tulip Honey*

## TUPELO HONEY

The Tupelo gum tree grows in many parts of the United States. Honey bees forage the blossoms flowering in both Black Tupelo and White Tupelo gum trees.

**Fig. 4.89** *Tupelo Flowers*

Fig. 4.90 *Tupelo Honey*

Black Tupelo honey is a darker honey that granulates quite easily. It is mainly used as a sweetener by bakers and confectioners.

White Tupelo honey is a clear honey with a golden or amber appearance and may have a green glow. It is a premium honey. It has a mild yet distinctive taste. It has a high fructose content making it sweeter than many other honeys so it may be used in smaller quantities. It does not crystallise easily. It is expensive as is considered to be a gourmet honey.

## USES

It is a table honey. It may be used on toast and on ice creams.

## ULMO HONEY

The Ulmo tree flourishes in the rainforests of Chile and yields a tasty and beneficial honey. Pretty white flowers bloom on these trees and attract a large number of bees who forage and gather nectar to manufacture a honey that is produced in Chile. The tree also imparts a natural floral fragrance which may be another factor that attracts the bees.

Fig. 4.91 *Ulmo Flower*

The Ulmo tree also grows in Argentina and Scotland. It has been successfully introduced in the North Pacific Coast of the United States of America.

Ulmo honey has an amber appearance. It has a delicate and sweet taste with buttery and floral overtones. It also has a delicate floral aroma.

## USES

It is considered to have medicinal value. It is used as an ingredient in food, in cosmetics and in medicine, especially by the natives in Chile and is gaining recognition in other parts of the world. It is used to treat skin infections and is also used in facial cleanser formulations. Research studies have shown that it may be used for wound healing.

Fig. 4.92 *Ulmo Honey*

Ulmo honey is used as a table honey. It may be used on toast, drizzled on baked goods, as an ingredient in puddings and also as a sweetener in sports drinks.

## VIPER'S BUGLOSS HONEY

Fig. 4.93 *Viper's Bugloss Flower*

Growing wildly in many parts of the world Viper's Bugloss or Blueweed is predominantly found in most parts of Europe, in Western Siberia, in New Zealand, in North America, in Western and Central Asia, in Sicily, in Sardinia, in the Mediterranean and in Chile. It is also called "blue borage" or simply "borage."

The flowers are initially pink but turn to a vivid and extremely attractive blue and honey bees and other insects pollinate it and draw nectar.

The honey has a dark amber or brown appearance. It has a subtle flavour with floral overtones. Sometimes it has a hint of vanilla notes. It crystallises slowly.

## USES

Viper's Bugloss is a popular table honey. It may be used on toast, on biscuits and on muffins. It is used to sweeten hot beverages including tea and coffee. It is also a good flavour to add to lemon based beverages including lemon tea. It may be paired with a wide variety of cheeses. It is a popular honey.

**Fig. 4.94** *Viper's Bugloss Honey*

## WILD THYME HONEY

Commonly obtained from North America, Greece and New Zealand Wild Thyme flourishes in specific regions including Croatia, Macedonia, Malta and North Africa. Fragrant Wild Thyme flowers bloom in spring covering mainly hills like an astounding purple natural carpet and attract honey bees in droves.

**Fig. 4.95** *Wild Thyme Flower*

The honey is deep, dark and intense. It has a dark caramel appearance. It has a strong and distinct flavour with wood and grass notes.

## USES

Wild Thyme honey is a great cooking honey and imparts an excellent flavour as an ingredient, in sauces in marinades and to meat dishes and fish dishes especially salmon and trout. It is also used to make salad dressings. It is used to flavour plain yogurt and is particularly popular in Greece where Greek Wild Thyme honey and yogurt is often a part of the breakfast. It is often used in baking as a sweetener and many biscuits and crumpets have this honey as an essential ingredient. It also pairs well with strong cheeses.

**Fig. 4.96** *Wild Thyme Honey*

Some other monofloral honeys that are not easily obtainable and more countries specific are lesser known but popular in niches. Durian honey from Malaysia is quite a strong honey. Soya bean honey may be obtained from various parts of the world. Brazilian Peppertree is very popular local honey with a rich vibrant flavour. Blackberry honey is produced in Ireland. However its taste is unique and not very popular and hence it is often blended with Clover honey. Carob honey is quite rare and has a unique flavour. It is dark amber in colour and crystallises easily. Dandelion honey is a rare honey produced in parts of Europe. It is strong and mildly sweet. It has a golden yellow to amber appearance.

Blackcurrant honey is not easily available and has a nice flavour. Mint honey as the name suggests is obtained from the flowers of various species of the mint family. It is rare to obtain and is more often a part of polyfloral or wildflower honey. It has a sweet taste with minty overtones.

Monofloral honeys are generally sold at a premium rate. Near infrared spectroscopy and other methods can be used to test the authenticity of monofloral honey.

## 3. POLYFLORAL HONEY

Polyfloral honey, as the name suggests, is honey that is made from the nectar of several flowers. It is also often called Wildflower honey. When gathered from forests it is called Wildflower honey. Bees may visit many different varieties of flowers. This is why polyfloral honey may differ significantly in aroma and flavour each year depending on various factors including the profusion of blossoms and the types of flowers the bee may have visited.

Polyfloral honey is more easily available when compared with monofloral honey. It is also cheaper than monofloral honey and may sometimes have a more easily acceptable taste, flavour and consistency as it is a natural blend of several blossoms.

## 4. HONEYDEW HONEY

Certain insects belonging to the order of insects - hemiptera, mainly aphids secrete honeydew and honey bees gather these secretions from plants and process it to form honey. This type of honey is called Honeydew honey. It

**Fig. 4.97** *Honeydew Honey*

is generally thicker and darker in colour when compared with floral honey. It is also less easily digestible. It has a strong taste and may or may not be the choice of all honey lovers. It has lesser amounts of simple sugars like glucose and fructose and larger amounts of complex sugars. It also has a higher content of minerals and a high antioxidant effect and antibacterial activity when compared with floral honeys.

Honeydew honey is obtained mainly from specific locations including the Black Forest in Germany; Greece, Bulgaria and Northern California. When compared with the rest of the world, it is more popular in Europe and Asia. It is important to harvest the honey before winter sets in as the cold weather causes health problems in bee colonies. It is necessary to maintain good bee keeping practices to obtain healthy and nutritious honeydew honey.

## PROCESSING AND PACKAGING METHODS

The types of honey, classified according to their processing and packaging methods, are as follows:

- a. Chunk honey
- b. Comb honey
- c. Crystallised honey
- d. Dried honey
- e. Pasteurised honey
- f. Raw honey
- g. Strained honey
- h. Ultrafiltered honey
- i. Ultrasonication honey
- j. Whipped honey

## CHUNK HONEY

When one or more pieces of comb honey are placed in jars containing extracted honey (in liquid form), it is called chunk honey. Chunk honey is a combination of extracted and comb honey and offers what some might see as the best of both worlds. The chunk of comb honey contains more propolis and pollen when compared with the extracted honey.

**Fig. 4.98** *Chunk Honey*

Chunk honey is generally packed in wide mouth glass jars so that one can see the honey combs floating in the liquid honey as well as easily extract the comb from the bottle.

## COMB HONEY

Comb honey is honey present in its original natural package namely the honey comb. It contains raw, fresh, natural unprocessed honey. It is also called section honey. Before honey extractors were invented, comb honey was the way in which honey was marketed.

**Fig. 4.99** *Comb Honey*

However, even after the advent of several modern inventions for extracting honey, without its comb, comb honey is still popular. It is much more expensive than extracted honey and is used in an "as is" form or added to extracted honey to make chunk honey. It has a better flavour, aroma and freshly available nutrients when compared with extracted honey.

Though many types of honeycombs are available throughout the year, it is better to use seasonal honeycombs. This product is fragile and tastes its best when fresh. It is advisable to store it at temperatures around 20 C to 30 C.

Many connoisseurs consider honey present naturally in its honeycomb to be the most attractive form of honey. Fresh comb honey's preferred use is to be spread on bread especially fresh bread, making it a delightful treat for one and all. The honey comb is edible and many consider it a crunchy accompaniment to the fresh bread. It may have been the replacement of chewing gum for our ancestors as it does have a chewy texture. It is also excellent when crushed over natural cut fruit including kiwis, grapefruit, apples or other fruits of your choice.

## CRYSTALLISED HONEY

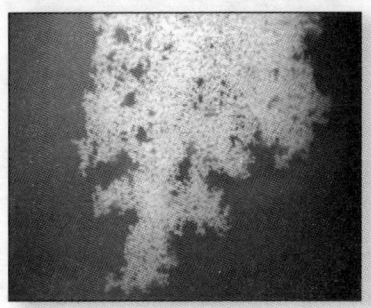

**Fig. 4.100** *Crystallised Honey*

Sometimes a part of the glucose present in honey spontaneously crystallises. To remove the crystals and restore the honey to its liquid state, it is necessary to stir the honey in a container containing water at a temperature of around 49C or 120 F.

Crystallised honey is also called granulated honey and is sometimes sold commercially. However, honey is dehydrated to make granulated honey which can be used just as one uses granulated sugar.

## DRIED HONEY

Dried honey products are generally used commercially. Liquid honey is drum dried, roller dried, spray dried or freeze dried.

It is available as crystals, granules, powder or flakes. Sometimes additives are added. When additives including starch, natural sweeteners, proteins, vitamins or fibres or in various food formulations are added as per specific client requirements, it is termed as a honey product rather than as pure honey. Dried honey may be used as an ingredient in various dry mixtures, as coatings or as a seasoning.

Dried honey is easier to pack and store commercially. It generally has a consistent colour and, flavour.

## PASTEURIZED HONEY

When honey is heated using pasteurisation, a process discovered by Louis Pasteur, it is called pasteurised honey. This process destroys yeast cells, keeps the honey in a liquid form and destroys microcrystallisation of cells. However excess heat also has detrimental effects as HMF (hydroxymethyl furfural) is formed in large quantities and this is undesirable. The action of the enzyme diastase is also reduced. Heat also affects the flavour, appearance and aroma of the honey and darkens the colour.

**Fig. 4.101** *Pasteurized Honey*

## RAW HONEY

Raw honey is the honey that is obtained in an "as in the beehive state" or obtained using extraction methods without the application of heat, though small amounts of heat are sometimes used. Raw honey may contain small bits and pieces of wax, propolis, active enzymes and some pollen.

Raw honey is, as the term suggests, the raw and natural form of honey obtained without processing or pasteurizing the product. It is said to be the healthiest choice among the different types of honey. It has a distinctive fresh aroma and nutrients at their optimum best. It is rich in bioflavonoids and antioxidants.

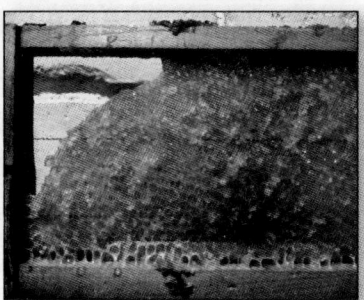

**Fig. 4.102** *Raw Honey*

Among all the different varieties of honey available in the market raw honey is said to have the best medicinal properties. Organic farms generally sell only raw honey. This honey commands a premium price in the market.

## STRAINED HONEY

When honey is strained through fine sieves to remove wax pieces, propolis and other particulate matter, the resultant honey is called strained honey. The honey comb is crushed and then strained through a fine mesh. This strained honey still contains the essential elements in honey including, pollen, enzymes, vitamins and minerals.

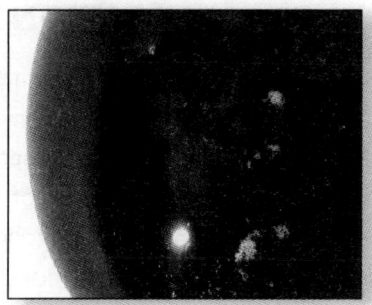

**Fig. 4.103** *Strained Honey*

Generally raw honey is strained as some customers do not like to find pieces of wax and other particulate matter in their honey.

## ULTRAFILTERED HONEY

To produce ultrafiltered honey, the honey is finely filtered under high pressure. This results in a product that has almost no particulate matter including any pollen grains or extraneous solids. It is heated before being passed through a fine filtration process. The result is liquid honey without crystals. This process increases the shelf life but also decreases the number of yeast cells and enzyme activity. The phytonutrient activity and enzyme activities are reduced due to high temperature and pressure. Hence some of its nutritive value is lost.

**Fig. 4.104** *Ultrafiltered Honey*

## ULTRASONICATION HONEY

Ultrasonication is an alternative process to treat honey. Instead of heat, ultrasonic waves are used to disintegrate the structure of the cells thus forming a clear liquid free flowing product that does not crystallise quickly. This process decreases the number of yeast cells considerably. It does decrease but does not totally eliminate the enzyme activity in honey.

**Fig. 4.105** *Ultrasonication Honey*

## WHIPPED HONEY

Whipped honey is known by several names including creamed honey, candied honey, churned honey, honey fondant and spun honey. The honey is processed so that small crystals that prevent the formation of larger crystals are formed in the honey. This processed honey has a smooth consistency and is easy to spread on any food surface. Whipped honey has a smooth creamy texture that is appreciated by some lovers of honey.

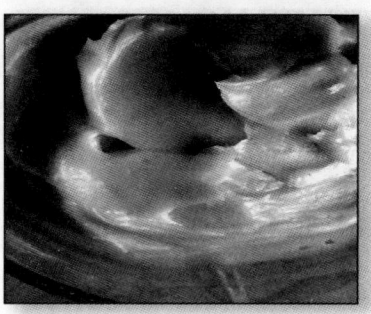

**Fig. 4.106** *Whipped Honey*

## SPECIALTY HONEYS AND HONEY PRODUCTS

There are a few special or different honey products available in the market. They include:
- Flavoured honey
- Fruit honey
- Infused honey
- Kosher honey
- Organic honey

## FLAVOURED HONEY

Flavoured honey is not a pure honey product. Certain flavours are added to honey. They may include herbs, spices and other flavouring substances including flavours like candy, vanilla, chocolate chip etc.

**Fig. 4.107** *Flavoured Honey*

## FRUIT HONEY

Fresh fruit and fruit extracts have been used to flavour honey. These honeys are different from monofloral honeys or single source honeys. In monofloral honeys nectar is obtained from the flowers or blossoms of a particular plant and is converted to honey by the honeybees. In fruit honeys the actual fruit is used to flavour the honey. Although almost any flavour may be used some of the more common fruit flavoured honey uses the following fruits:

**Fig. 4.108** Fruit Honey

- Apricots
- Blackberries
- Blueberries
- Cherries
- Lemons
- Mangoes
- Orange
- Peaches
- Raspberries
- Strawberries
- Tangerines

## INFUSED HONEY

Sometimes honeys are steeped in herbs and spices to add unique and specific flavours. These honeys are called infused honeys.

## KOSHER HONEY

Pure raw honey is considered to be kosher honey. However, to ensure that is it kosher it needs to be certified.

## ORGANIC HONEY

Organic honey is the honey that is produced using stringent requirements needed to classify it as organic. Although there may not be enough proof that the bees have only collected nectar from organic flowers, the producers ensure that the bees are not given antibiotics to protect them from diseases. There are sufficient and stringent stipulations and guidelines on the origin of honey bees and the site of the apiaries (certified to be organic land with organic crops etc) to ensure that honey is organic.

**Fig. 4.109** *Organic Honey*

There have not been any studies proving that organic honey is better for consumption. However, it is generally safer to consume any organic foods as indiscriminate use of pesticides, antibiotics etc. may have just become a norm. Some agriculturists worldwide seem to be quite interested in increasing immediate yields rather than offering sustainable benefits. Sufficient studies on the long term use of pesticides, antibiotics etc on honey are not available as yet.

## GRADES OF HONEY

Depending on the water content, the flavour and aroma, the absence of defects and the clarity honey is graded as Grade A, Grade B, Grade C and Grade D or substandard honey, with Grade A being the best quality of honey available.

- An A grade honey generally has a moisture content that it less than 18.6%. It has a good aroma and flavour. If it is a monofloral honey it should have the characteristic aroma and flavour of its source. It has no visible defects and a clear appearance.
- A B grade honey has a moisture content that is less than 18.6%. It has a reasonably good aroma and flavour. It is reasonably free from visible defects and reasonably clear.
- A C grade honey has a moisture content that is less than 20%. It has a fairly good flavour and aroma. It is fairly free of visible defects. It has a fairly clear appearance.
- A D grade or substandard honey has moisture content below 20%. It fails all the criteria of Grade C as far as flavour, aroma, absence of defects and clarity is concerned.

## PFUND SCALE

Honey may also be graded as per the Pfund Scale. It is a grading system where the colour of the honey is correlated with standards measured in millimeters.

The Pfund colour grader consists of a wedge shaped amber glass with a wedge shaped cell next to it. The cell is filled with the honey sample. A visual reading is taken. The distance in millimeters the wedge is moved to match with the sample is calculated.

As per US Standards, the colour range is measured as follows. This range may differ slightly when compared with the scales used in Canada and Australia.

| Colour | Pfund scale in mm |
|---|---|
| Water white | < 9 |
| Extra white | 9-17 |
| White | 18-34 |
| Extra light amber | 35-50 |
| Light amber | 51-85 |
| Amber | 86-114 |
| Dark amber | > 114 |

# 5

# PRESERVING HONEY

To preserve honey, there is no specific method to be followed. In fact decades old and even centuries old honey is still fit for human consumption though it may have antique rather than edible value.

However, decreasing humidity levels are beneficial for maintaining the quality of honey. The sugar content in honey is high enough to prevent fermentation. In humid conditions, when moisture gets added to honey, the sugar content decreases leading to increased yeast activity and fermentation. It is also important not to expose honey to high temperatures or to oxidation.

High temperatures around 37° C decrease the nutrient content of the honey. As the temperature increases to around 40° C, there is destruction of the enzyme invertase and at temperatures around 50° C the honey begins to caramelise.

Crystallisation is a common property in honeys. Even when honey is properly stored, one may see some crystallisation. Temperature (around 10° to 20° C), seeds to form crystals, trace compounds and a specific mixture of certain sugars facilitate the formation of crystals. This process of crystallisation may be reversed by gently heating honey preferably on a water bath, double boiler or Bain Marie. Try to heat honey indirectly by placing it over hot water. Using the microwave to heat honey is inadvisable as the amount of HMF hydroxymethylfurfural (an undesirable natural substance) increases when honey is heated to high temperatures.

**Fig. 5.1** Honey in Ceramic Jar

In olden times honey used to be packed in ceramic jars or wooden jars. The honey sometimes took up the characteristics of the wood. Currently glass and plastic are the favoured methods of packing honey. As nature intended, the honeycomb is the best place to preserve honey.

# USES OF HONEY

As with most natural foods, to a large extent, the health benefits of honey depend on the quality of the honey. Depending on its use – as a food (sweetener), as a cosmetic or as a medicine, its use and its affordability are the main factors that may go into choosing the type of honey.

## AS A FOOD

Honey has been a natural sweetener through the ages. Once ancient humankind learnt to harvest this delicacy from hollow trees, rocks and crevices – they began to use this natural sweetener both as a food and as a medicine.

Mention of honey in religious texts increased its value and with progress, the nutritional value of honey was also calculated thus expanding its value not just for its taste but also for its healing nature.

In every continent, be it the Americas, Africa, Asia, Europe or down to Australia, honey has been consumed by its citizens from time immemorial. In fact, it is a fairly ancient food that is still produced by traditional as well as modern methods.

It is sad that some unscrupulous apiarists feed honey bees a dilute sugar solution to manufacture honey. Organic or wild honey may just be the best form of honey as it will preserve the natural goodness of honey without taking away any of its minute but essential nutrients. For cooking, free flowing honey is preferred but as a natural food raw honey with all its goodness intact as nature meant it to be may be the best way to consume it.

Honey predominantly contains easily digestible sugars such as glucose and fructose. It also contains some complex sugars, vitamins, minerals, amino acids, enzymes, bioflavonoids and antioxidants all of which promote good health. As a natural food honey is indeed a boon as a sweetener when compared with other natural sweeteners that are generally more energy yielding substances rather than healthy substances. Honey not only provides energy but also provides a few essential nutrients albeit in small amounts.

Honey also lends itself as a natural sweetener in various food formulations and recipes. It adds taste as a unique glaze, as a sauce or even in powder form to make some food formulations and supplements more palatable and healthy.

Honey is used as an essential ingredient to add sweetness to many dishes and recipes prepared worldwide. It has been a common ingredient in foods from the ages. It also is used as a 'gourmet' ingredient in modern and trendy cooking.

There are so many recipes that use honey as an ingredient. It would take several cookery books to fill with recipes including honey as a major or minor ingredient. It is important to note that generally honey is sweeter than sugar and when it is used as a substitute for sugar the quantity should be reduced when compared with sugar. Honey also browns faster when compared with sugar. Hence cooking and baking temperatures may be lowered when using honey.

# Uses of Honey

In its simplest forms it is used as follows:
- To sweeten beverages mainly tea
- As a drizzle over apple or other fruit slices with or without a smidgeon of cinnamon
- To sweeten plain yogurt
- As a filling with peanut butter and bananas
- With milk/soya milk and chocolate as a milk shake

Alternatively, it is used as an ingredient to prepare sauces, marinades, glazes and spreads.

Honey can be used as an ingredient to prepare each course of an entire meal. It can be used to make
- A starter
- A main dish
- A side dish
- A snack
- A drink
- A dessert

Honey is very versatile in its use. It may be used as a part of any and every meal. Whether you add it on bread, have it with cereal, spread it on a chapatti or dosa, or make it as a side dish accompanying your main dish at breakfast, it is a pleasant addition.

On a lazy day when you decide to have brunch, you may have a honey dish together with many other of your easy to make or favourite foods.

It may be used as the main dish for your lunch or even as a side dish or accompaniment.

In the evening snacking time may be a honey treat with sandwiches with a honey filling, donuts glazed in honey, honey roasted nuts, or any dessert including pastries and cake.

Honey can also form a part of your dinner. Perhaps you can have a glass of mead to celebrate an occasion. You may finally retire for the night after mixing a tablespoon of honey in your glass of milk or soya milk.

Many industries also use honey as an essential ingredient in their commercial formulations. The major food industries which use honey as a food ingredient include:

- Baked goods
- Breakfast cereals
- Confectionary
- Ice cream
- Jam and marmalades
- Snack bars
- Spreads and sauces

# HONEY RECIPES

## APPETISERS / STARTERS RECIPE

### CHEESE/HONEY DIP WITH FRESH FRUIT

**Ingredients**

Cream cheese 1 packet

Honey ¼ cup

Cinnamon powder ¼ th tsp

Lemon juice (freshly squeezed) 1 tbsp

Vanilla 1 tsp

Almonds ¼ cup

Fresh fruit slices

**Method**

Lightly toast the almonds and chop them finely. Take a bowl. Add the cream cheese and beat it till it is light and fluffy. Now add vanilla, lemon juice and cinnamon and mix it well. Top it with almonds. Serve the dip by placing it in a serving bowl surrounded by cut fruits in a large platter.

You may serve fruit slices of apples, bananas, strawberries, peaches, nectarines, grapes or any other fruit of your choice.

## SPICY HONEY VEGETABLE DIP

**Ingredients**

Mayonnaise (preferably low fat) 1 cup
Honey 1 cup
Vinegar (preferably white wine) 1 tbsp
Red chilli powder ¼ tsp
Coriander powder ¼ tsp
Turmeric powder a pinch
Garam masala powder a pinch
Salt to taste
Pepper powder to taste

**Method**

Combine together the mayonnaise, honey, vinegar, spice powders, salt and pepper and refrigerate for approximately one hour. Serve this dip with an assortment of freshly cut vegetables. You may include celery, carrots, cauliflower, broccoli, cucumber and any other vegetables of your choice. If you don't have individual spice powders you may use ¾ to 1 tsp of curry powder instead.

## SALADS

## STRAWBERRY AND HONEY SALAD

**Ingredients**

For the salad
Strawberries 250 gm
Lettuce 250 gm
For the vinegar and honey dressing
White vinegar 2 tbsp

Olive oil 1 tbsp
Honey ½ tbsp
Salt to taste
Pepper to taste

**Method**

Wash the strawberries in clean water and slice them. Cut the lettuce into pieces. Place them in a bowl.

In another bowl whisk together the olive oil, white vinegar and honey. Add salt and pepper to taste.

Combine the cut fruit and vegetables with the dressing. Toss the strawberries and lettuce till they get coated with the dressing.

Serve.

You may also try other fruit and vegetable combinations if you wish.

## BAKED POTATO SALAD TOPPED WITH A HONEY AND MAYONNAISE DRESSING

**Ingredients**

Baby new potatoes 1 kg
Red pepper 1
Red onion 1
Parsley a few sprigs
Mayonnaise 1 cup
Sour cream 1 cup
Garlic 2 cloves
Honey 1 tbsp
Mustard (optional) 1 tsp
Salt to taste

### Method

Cut the potatoes into halves and bake them in a preheated oven around 200C for around 30 to 40 minutes till they are tender. Cool it.

When the potatoes are getting baked, finely dice the bell peppers. Chop the onions and parsley. Crush the garlic.

Take a bowl add the mayonnaise, bell peppers, onions, parsley, honey, garlic and mustard if desired. Mix all these ingredients together. Add some salt if required. Combine the potatoes with this mixture.

For a better appearance instead of mixing in the potatoes, you may also top each individual half of the baked potatoes with the prepared mixture and serve.

## MAIN DISH RECIPES

## QUINOA AND TEMPEH WITH A HONEY AND SESAME SAUCE

### Ingredients

Quinoa 6 tbsp

Carrots 2

Water ¾ cup

Rice vinegar 1 tbsp

Sesame seeds 1 tbsp

Sesame oil 2 tbsp

Tempeh 1 packet (8ounces /225 grams)

Spring onion (green onion/scallion) 1

Honey 1 ½ tbsp

Soy sauce 3 tsp

Cornstarch ½ tsp

Water 1 tbsp

**Method**

Rinse the quinoa in water. Take a small saucepan. Add ¾ cup of water and bring to a boil. Add the rinsed quinoa and when it starts boiling reduce the flame to simmer. Cook for about for about 10-12 minutes with a closed lid. Uncover it and let it stand.

Toast the sesame seeds in a dry skillet. Grate the carrots. Take a bowl and combine together the grated carrot, the sesame seeds, the rice vinegar, half the quantity of sesame oil and half the quantity of soya sauce in a bowl. Keep it aside.

Crumble the tempeh into bite sized pieces. Heat the other half of the sesame oil (1 tbsp) in a skillet and add the tempeh pieces. Brown it for about 7-8 minutes.

Make a honey sauce by combining together the honey, the other half of the soya sauce (1 ½ tsp), one tbsp water and the cornstarch in a pan and cook till the sauce thickens. Add the tempeh pieces to this sauce so they get coated with it.

Finally slice the spring onion and divide it into two portions.

Divide the quinoa, the carrot mixture and the tempeh mixture into two portions each.

Take two bowls. Fill the bottom of each bowl with one portion quinoa, then add the carrot mixture and the quinoa mixture and finally top each bowl with the spring onions and serve.

## MEAT BALLS GLAZED WITH HONEY AND GARLIC

**Ingredients**

Meat 1 kg

Eggs 2

Dried bread crumbs 1 cup

Milk ¾ cup

Ketchup ¾ cup

Honey ½ cup

Soya sauce 3tbsp

Red onion big 1

Butter 1 tbsp

Garlic 4 cloves

Salt to taste

**Method**

Mince the meat finely. Finely chop the onions in a large bowl. Break the eggs into it and add the milk. Then add the minced meat and onions and salt. Mix it well and shape it into one inch balls.

Grease two baking pans and put the balls in these pans. Bake it uncovered at 204° C for about 15 minutes till the meat loses its pinkness.

When the meatballs are in the oven you can start making the sauce by taking a saucepan and add the butter. Sauté crushed garlic in the butter till it gets tender. Now add the ketchup, honey, soya sauce and bring this mixture to a boil. Then reduce the flame to simmer and cook for about 5 minutes.

Drain the meat balls and add it to the simmering sauce. Keep stirring the meat balls till each one gets coated with the sauce. Cook for about 8-10 minutes till the meatball is cooked and serve.

Any meat including poultry meat may be used.

Vegetarians may make vegetable balls using mixed vegetables and add them to the sauce. Paneer may be added to the vegetable balls or may be used to make paneer balls.

## SIDE DISH RECIPES

### HONEY GLAZED CARROTS

*Ingredients*
Carrots 6
Honey 3tbsp
Vegetable oil 1 tbsp
Lemon juice ½ tsp
Salt to taste

*Method*
Slice the carrots and boil them in salted water. You can also steam the carrots if you wish.

Remove and drain away excess water if any.

Take a thick pan and add the honey, oil and lemon juice add the carrots and cook for a couple of minutes till the honey/oil/lemon juice mixture coats the carrots and gives it a glaze.

Serve.

Please note that carrots may be substituted with other vegetables including sweet potatoes or onions. You may also get a bit adventurous and add a smidgeon of cinnamon/cardamom or even dried ginger powder.

### SWEET POTATOES GLAZED WITH HONEY

*Ingredients*
Sweet potatoes (medium sized) 6
Honey ½ cup
Pineapple juice ½ cup
Brown sugar ½ cup

White sugar ½ cup

Butter 3tbsp

Orange or lemon zest 1 tbsp

Ground ginger ½ tsp

Ground cardamom ½ tsp

**Method**

Wash the sweet potatoes and put them in a pan of cold water. Ensure that the water covers the sweet potatoes. Heat the pan. When the water boils reduce the flame and simmer for approximately 20 minutes till the sweet potatoes are firm yet tender.

Take a pan and combine together honey, pineapple juice, brown and white sugar, the zest of your choice, the ginger and cardamom powder. Bring to a boil, then simmer and cook for about 15 minutes.

Peel the sweet potatoes and cut them into thick slices. Put these slices in the honey pineapple and spice mixture. Toss it carefully and see that all the sweet potato slices are glazed. Cook for about 25 minutes on low heat in an uncovered pan until all the potatoes are evenly glazed.

Serve hot

## SNACK RECIPES

### DATE AND CHOCOLATE BARS

*Ingredients*

Pitted dates 225 gm

Chocolate pieces 1 cup

Honey ¾ cup

Flour 1 ¼ cup

Rolled oats ½ cup

Chopped nuts 1 cup

Soft butter ¼ cup

Eggs 2

Baking soda 1 ¼ tsp

Vanilla 1 tsp

Salt ½ tsp

Hot water 1 and ¼ cup

**Method**

Chop the dates and simmer it in a pan along with one teaspoon of soda for 10 minutes. Let it cool.

Sift the flour with the salt and ¼ tsp of baking soda. In a mixing bowl, combine the honey and butter till it becomes fluffy. Now add each egg and beat it well. Add the flour mixture to the mixing bowl and blend it in thoroughly. Now stir in the date mixture, vanilla, rolled oats and half of the mini chocolate pieces.

Grease a baking tray and spread this mixture. Sprinkle the rest of the chocolate pieces and chopped nuts on the top of the spread.

Bake in an oven at 175° C for 35 minutes. Cool it and cut it into bars or squares.

Serve individually or top it with vanilla ice cream or honey sweetened whipped cream.

## CHOCOLATE AND WALNUT FUDGE

### Ingredients

Semi sweet chocolate chips 400 gm

Bitter sweet chocolate 100 gm

Sweetened condensed milk 1 can (around 414 ml)
Walnuts 1 cup
Honey ½ cup
Salt ¼ tsp

**Method**

Crumble the bitter chocolate to coarse bits. Coarsely chop the walnuts.

Take a saucepan. Add the honey, sweetened condensed milk and salt and mix it well. With constant stirring, bring this mixture to a boil. Lower it to simmer and then add the bitter chocolate bits and chocolate chips. Keep stirring constantly until the chocolate melts and becomes a smooth mixture. Now add the chopped walnuts and pour immediately into a pre greased 8'x 8" pan which is lined with foil and has been greased with butter. Smooth the mixture on the pan especially the top.

Let it cool and refrigerate it till it becomes cold. Cut into pieces of your optional choice.

## BEVERAGE RECIPES

## HONEY DRINK (IDEAL AS A BREAKFAST DRINK)

### Ingredients

Milk 2 cups
Banana (large, ripe) 1
Orange juice ½ cup
Honey ½ cup
Milk powder (low fat) ¼ cup
Wheat germ ¼ cup
Ice cubes 5

### Method

Blend together all the ingredients except the ice cubes, till you obtain a smooth mixture. Then add the ice cubes and blend again.

Serve immediately.

## BANANA SMOOTHIE

### Ingredients

Bananas (medium, ripe) 2

Milk 1 ½ cup

Yogurt 1 cup

Honey ¼ cup

Vanilla 1 tsp

Ground cinnamon 1 pinch

Ice cubes 5

### Method

Combine together the bananas, milk, yogurt, honey, vanilla and cinnamon and blend it in a blender till smooth. Now add the ice cubes one at a time and blend.

Serve immediately.

## HONEY CITRUS SOOTHER

### Ingredients

Tea bags (green or black) 3

Grapefruit juice 1 cup

Honey ¼ cup

Cinnamon stick 1

Boiling water 3 cups

**Method**

Take a tea pot and place the tea bags and cinnamon stick inside. Add the boiling water. Steep it for about 5 minutes. Remove the tea bags and cinnamon stick. Stir in the grapefruit juice and honey.

Serve hot.

## HONEY LEMON QUENCHER

**Ingredients**

Honey ½ cup

Lemon juice ¼ cup

Salt ½ tsp or to taste

Water 7 ½ cups

**Method**

Combine all the ingredients together and serve.

Please note that using lukewarm water to dissolve honey hastens the process.

# DESSERT RECIPES

## ALMOND AND HONEY CRUNCH

**Ingredients**

Cornflakes 2 ½ cup

Almonds 1 cup

Honey ¼ cup

Butter 1 tbsp

Orange peel 1 tbsp

**Method**

Cut the almonds into thin slivers. Grate the orange peel. Combine together all the ingredients in a thick frying pan and cover on a low heat. Constantly stir the mixture till the almonds turn golden brown. Now remove it from the heat and add the cornflakes.

Spread this mixture on a buttered baking sheet. When it gets cooled, break it into pieces of your desired size.

## CHIFFON HONEY CAKE

*Ingredients*

Eggs 6

Flour 2 cups

Honey 1 cup

Brewed strong hot coffee ¾ cup

Walnuts ¾ cup

Sugar ½ cup

Vegetable oil ½ cup

Instant coffee granules 1 tbsp

Baking soda 1 tsp

Baking powder 1 tsp

Cream of tartar ½ tsp

Cinnamon ½ tsp

Cloves ½ tsp

Nutmeg ½ tsp

Salt ¼ tsp

*Method*

Add the instant coffee granules to the strongly brewed coffee. Mix it well. Add the baking soda to it and keep it aside.

Separate the egg yolks from the egg whites. Beat the egg whites in a bowl while adding the cream of tartar until the mixture becomes stiff.

Mix the rest of the ingredients in another bowl together with the coffee mixture till a smooth batter is obtained. Now carefully fold in the egg whites.

Pour the batter into an ungreased baking tray. Bake it at 178° C for about an hour.

Insert a cake tester to the centre of the cake to confirm that it is evenly and well cooked. Cool it thoroughly and then remove the cake from the pan.

Serve.

# 8

# AS A COSMETIC

It has been an established fact that our ancestors considered honey to be beneficial for the skin. Honey is said to have a moisturising and softening action on the skin. It may improve the suppleness and elasticity of the skin showing up as smoothness and radiating health.

Whether it is used as a general healer or for specific conditions or problems, it acts as a natural antiseptic and cleaning agent. Together with other natural ingredients, it has been used for many purposes including getting rid of blemishes and spots, as a face pack, as a cleansing agent and even as a quick fix facelift.

Honey has several uses in the cosmetic industry. It is used to make

- Face masks
- To soften the hands
- In soaps
- In shampoos
- In skin creams

## HONEY IN FACE MASKS

Honey has been considered as a skin softener. It is said that honey moisturises and rejuvenates skin. Honey is generally used in combination with other natural substances to make face masks whether in the cosmetic industry or at home.

There are various combinations of face masks available in the market. There are also a few simple formulations using honey with different substances and some of them are listed below.

Always remember that some human beings are prone to allergies and each individual may respond differently to different substances whether ingested or applied topically. If you find any adverse reactions please stop using any face mask whether cosmetic or homemade immediately.

## FACE MASK 1 (MAY BE SUITABLE FOR DRY AND NORMAL SKIN)

Honey 1 tbsp

Olive oil 1 tsp

Egg yolk 1

Cucumber 2 slices

Mix the honey and olive oil in a bowl. Now add the egg yolk and cream this mixture. Apply on the face for around 20 minutes, avoiding eyes.

It is advisable to wipe the face initially with a warm towel or to steam gently. After this process the honey mask is applied. Finally the eyes are covered with 2 slices of cucumber and the individual relaxes for about 20 minutes. Then the mixture is wiped or washed off the face using warm water. Finally cold water, which is supposed to close the pores, is splashed on the face.

If you feel your skin feels better and there is a light glow, the honey mask has had a good effect. For oily skin it is preferable to use the white of the egg and not the yolk.

## FACE MASK 2 (MAY BE SUITABLE FOR OILY SKIN)

Lemon juice ½ tsp

Honey 2 tbsp

Mix the honey with the lemon juice and apply gently on the face, avoiding eyes. Leave it on the face for about 20 minutes and wash the face with cold water.

## FACE MASK 3 (MAY BE SUITABLE FOR ALL TYPES OF SKIN)

Powdered oats 2 tsp

Honey 1 tsp

Mix the honey and oats together and apply gently on the face, avoiding eyes. Keep the face mask on for about 15 minutes and wash gently with cold water.

## FACE MASK 4

Fruit pulp 3 tbsp

Honey 1 tsp

Mix the fruit pulp with the honey and apply gently over the face, avoiding eyes. Wipe the mixture after 20 minutes and wash the face with cold water.

Generally apple, banana, strawberries or papaya pulp is used.

You may try any other fruit combinations which may suit your skin.

Please note that an individual can also be allergic to natural products including fruits so it always better to do a patch test on the skin. If you have acne prone skin please be extra careful as some ingredients may increase acne flare ups.

## TO SOFTEN THE HANDS

Generally, a small amount of honey is gently rubbed on the hands to soften them. If possible let the honey remain on the surface of the hands for about fifteen minutes and then wash your hands. Some people add a small amount of olive oil together with honey especially when the skin on the hands feels dry.

Sometimes honey is used in combination with other ingredients.

## HAND SOFTENER 1 FOR DRY AND ROUGH HANDS

Almond oil 2 tbsp

Honey 1 tsp

Egg yolk 1

Thoroughly mix all the three ingredients together. Massage the mixture gently into your hands. Keep it for about half an hour and then wash with clean water.

## HAND SOFTENER 2

Honey 1 tsp

Orange juice 1 tsp

Combine the honey and fresh orange juice together and very gently massage the mixture into your hands. Wash your hands with warm water after ten minutes and then with clear water. Pat dry and if you feel a difference you can continue this simple treatment.

## HAND SOFTENER 3

Honey 1 tsp

Wheat germ oil 1 tsp

Blend both the ingredients together and apply on the back of the hands. Keep it on for about fifteen minutes and wash your hands with clean water.

## HAND SOFTENER 4

Honey 1 tsp

Grape seed oil 1 tsp

Combine together the honey and grape seed oil. Apply this mixture on the hands. After fifteen minutes, wash your hands with clean water.

## IN SOAPS

Honey has been used an ingredient to make soaps. Whether commercially manufactured or homemade, honey imparts a lot of desirable characteristics to soaps including a pleasant scent and extra lathering capacity, which is quite an important requirement in soaps, as we are conditioned to think that a good lather means the cleaning is effective.

Together with honey, other skin friendly ingredients are used to make natural soaps. Various vegetable oils are used to make such soaps. Most often no artificial colours, fragrances and additives are used when making such soaps. Due to the honey used, these soaps may have some action on microbes and reduce the bacterial and fungal contamination on the hands. They not only clean the hands but also leave them with a smoother feeling.

It is possible to make soaps with honey as an ingredient at home. However, it is not as simple as just combining the ingredients, but you can try them out if you wish using soap making kits for homemade soaps and add honey judiciously as an ingredient. There are a wide variety of commercially available soaps that use honey as an ingredient.

## IN SHAMPOOS

Honey has been used as a natural conditioner and cleanser. It gives shine to the hair and may also lighten it over a period of time. Unless you are allergic to honey and/or pollen, it may be used on normal, dry, damaged or chemically treated hair.

One of the simplest homemade formulations is to combine two natural products – honey and bee pollen. Both these products are easily available and can be combined together to make a natural shampoo that leaves your hair more often than not, soft and shiny after every wash.

Honey and egg have been used traditionally from years to add bounce and shine to hair. Other ingredients are also added with these basic components.

A combination of milk and honey is also commonly used not only to clean but also to condition hair. The simplest method to use this mixture is to lightly whisk together the above ingredients and gently wash your hair with the mixture.

Some people prefer combining aloe vera with honey to make their own homemade shampoos. This combination is said to suit all kinds of hair types whether hair is dry, oily or normal. It is also a common commercial formulation available in shops that sell natural products.

There are also a few other natural compounds that are added together with honey to make natural shampoos. One shampoo formulation includes honey and hibiscus extract. Another formulation that includes honey and oatmeal is considered to be a good treatment for chemically damaged hair.

Whatever the combination may be, do check and see that you suffer from no allergies or any side effects, when you use a new formulation of shampoo whether it is based on natural or artificial substances as all substances have a chemical nature.

## IN SKIN CREAMS

Some people find it a bit messy to use honey directly on their skins. Keeping this fact in mind and also considering ease of use, many cosmetic manufacturers have formulated skin creams for various purposes. Thus, by making honey based creams, its natural goodness is kept intact while eliminating its sticky texture.

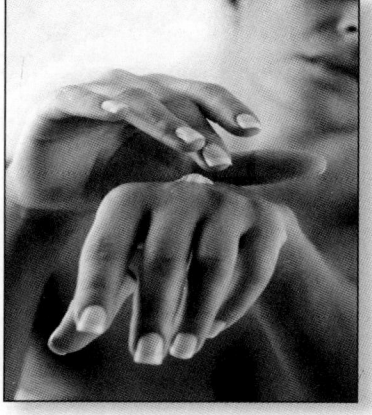

Honey based creams find use as moisturising creams,

**Fig. 8.1 Honey** used as a Hand Softener

hand softeners, hand sanitisers, anti wrinkle creams and also as topical antiseptics. They may be used as body lotions or creams all over the body, on the face, on the hands and feet and over dry areas like the knees and elbows. Rinse away the cream preferably using warm water to remove any feeling of stickiness.

Honey is generally non allergenic. However, some individuals are susceptible to allergies caused by honey and its products. Please stop usage if you find you are allergic to honey or any of the other products manufactured by honey bees.

# 9

# AS A MEDICINE

How does honey actually work as a medicine? A lot of research has been carried out to answer this question. Simply put, honey has the ability to inhibit the growth of microorganisms.

The antibacterial factors responsible for honey being considered to have antibacterial action include:
- The osmotic effect of its sugars
- Its pH and the presence of honey acids
- Hydrogen peroxide
- Other factors including the presence of phenols, proteins and undetermined factors

Some research studies have also shown that honey has antiviral and antiparasitic action. A few others studies have shown that honeys have antifungal activity against certain fungi.

Honey also acts as a natural antioxidant. Darker honeys are generally higher in phenols and have a higher activity.

Honey acts as a natural antiinflammatory agent and has shown lots of promise especially in wound healing.

## IN WESTERN MEDICAL SYSTEMS

It has been a well known fact from millennia that not only honey has high potential as a medicine but also has been proven to be a cure for several infections and ailments. It did not need sophisticated research for our ancestors to understand the importance of this useful substance. Although honey has gained international approval to treat wounds, as a dressing by the Western world, it has been traditionally been used to treat wounds from over five thousand years.

Modern research on medical grade honey has proven it to be an effective antidote and cure for several ailments. Recent research, including that conducted in 2010, has thrown up more facts on the potency of honey. Some researchers have isolated the protein named defensin1, from medical grade honey. This potential antibacterial factor present in honey will improve its use as a treatment for burns and skin infections. It has the potential for being part of future combinations of new antibacterial formulations. As more research is conducted humankind is gaining greater insights into the immune system of honey bees. This will lead to the breeding of healthier and stronger honey bees and hopefully create a synergistic relationship between humankind and nature which will be less exploitative and more complementary.

Thousands of years ago our ancestors knew that honey was useful in healing wounds. Ayurveda texts, ancient tribal medicine, etc. often applied honey on wounds. Much later, the western systems of medicine, caught up with its use of honey as a medicine. Since honey is not a patentable product unfortunately less research has been carried out and hence the modern world may be losing out on some of its natural antibacterial properties. Western systems of medicines dominate healing and curing of humans worldwide and it would be a boon for humankind if these systems conducted more research on the various benefits of honey.

Many research studies have been carried out on the use of honey as medicine using MGH or Medical Grade Honey. While

MGH is more expensive, clinical trials have shown that it is very effective in wound healing. However, even honeys bought from super markets proved to be effective though to a lesser extent when compared with MGH. In a comparative study of different types of honeys it was shown that honeys available from British supermarkets were potential sources of pathogenic organisms though there was no evidence of direct infection as a result of the presence of these microorganisms. However it was felt that vulnerable populations may suffer from the adverse effects of these microorganisms. Hence sterile honey products of good quality, which are available, are preferred for use as the benefits from proprietary products using sterile honey is much higher and safer.

Several studies have been carried out on the efficacy of honey for healing wounds, some studies have shown that honey may replace conventional therapies while others have considered it to be an alternative or complementary method of treatment depending on the types of wounds and the types of diseases or conditions to be treated.

Honey has been used effectively to treat coughs from time immemorial. Many homemakers and studies constantly reiterate the use of honey as a soother to relive cough symptoms and improve the quality of sleep at night. In a recent study, 105 children were administered with either honey, honey flavoured Dextromethorphan or no treatment. The result of the study showed that the treatment with honey gave the best results. Parents rated the treatment with honey as the best, as it gave relief from nocturnal cough and decreased the difficulty in sleep due to the infection in the upper respiratory tract.

There has been some research undertaken on the efficacy of honey with regard to oral wellness and dental health.

Most of the work done so far has been mainly in the form of pilot studies. One such study conducted using Manuka honey, found that there was a reduction in plaque formation and in bleeding sites in the gums. Therefore, this honey may be used in confectionery to treat periodontal diseases and gingivitis. However the fact that honey loses its antimicrobial properties at high temperatures and its overall antimicrobial effects are reduced above certain temperatures is a point that must be noted by confectionary manufacturers. More research and large studies have to be undertaken to confirm the use of honey to treat dental diseases.

Honey may also prove to have potential as an antiinfective treatment for a wide range of periodontal diseases. It may also prove to be effective in treating mouth ulcers and also to treat wounds that may develop after extraction of teeth or other types of oral surgery. Selecting honeys which have high antibacterial activity may also reduce the risk of developing dental caries that may be caused by the use of honey as a sweetener as simple and complex sugars present in honey have been implicated as a cause of dental caries.

Honey is also one of the best ways to boost energy levels. It is an instant energy fix that provides calories along with small amounts of vitamins, minerals and antioxidants. It is a tasty and healthy way to decrease tiredness.

## IN ALTERNATIVE MEDICINE

### IN AYURVEDA

Honey is called 'Madhu" in ayurveda. It is used to improve both physical and mental well being. Extensively used in many ayurvedic preparations, honey is revered as a natural ingredient in these preparations though certain strict guidelines are followed with reference to its use.

There are eight different kinds of honeys as per this system of medicine and the type depends on the type of bee collecting nectar from flowers. It has various uses depending on the type of honey.

As per Ayurveda, specific honeys may be used by itself or in combination with other natural ingredients including herbs and spices to treat various different diseases and conditions. Different combinations of honey with specific herbs or spices and condiments are used by ayurveda practitioners for the following treatments:

- As an instant energizer
- To heal tissues
- As a sedative
- To treat bed wetting disorders
- To restore damaged skin
- To quench thirst
- To stop hiccups
- To clean and heal wounds
- To improve eyesight
- To increase bodyweight
- As a mild laxative
- To treat coughs and colds
- To control blood pressure
- To relieve asthma
- To strengthen the heart muscles
- To purify blood
- To clear the sinuses

- To decrease infertility
- To treat diarrrhoea
- To treat nausea
- To treat vomiting
- To treat urinary tract disorders
- To eliminate intestinal worms
- To increase hair growth

When used as an ingredient for ayurvedic treatment it is necessary to note that certain precautions must be followed. They include:

- Honey must not be heated.
- Honey must not be mixed with hot and spicy foods.
- Honey must not be taken with fermented beverages.
- Honey must not be mixed with rain water.

If any untoward symptoms may occur while trying out these common ayurvedic remedies, it is always advisable to consult a registered ayurvedic doctor immediately. Before embarking on self treatment it may be always advisable to consult qualified personnel.

## IN HOMEOPATHY

Although honey is used in several homeopathic formulations especially cough related medications, it is perhaps the honey bee or apis that is used as an ingredient in several homeopathic formulations.

Bee and bee products are used by homeopaths to treat the following conditions:

- To treat skin complaints including hives (urticaria), bites, stings and itchy skin
- To treat oedema

- To treat urinary tract infections
- To treat certain types of fevers
- To treat headaches
- To treat arthritis
- To treat pleurisy
- Peritonitis

## IN AFRICAN MEDICINE

Honey has been in the African continent from time immemorial as a natural sweetener and healer. The ancient Egyptians used honey for various conditions and treatments including treating and healing wounds with honey. This practice is followed to date and the use of honey in wound healing is the forefront among all research on honey. The Egyptians also embalmed bodies using honey.

African holistic methods of treatment are still a common part of current day treatment by many tribes in the continent. Many of these methods have existed from millennia without documentation and modern researchers are currently documenting these commonly used ancient remedies. What was known by the ancient herbalists and healers is finding a place in the modern world. The most common ancient African system of medicine is called Yorubic or Orisha medicine. This system believes in the wholeness of the body in terms of food, exercise, rest and mental wellbeing. Honey is said to contribute to this wholeness.

Ancient African wisdom on honey is finding its place in the modern world, with extensive research on this natural and tasty sweetener. It is a well-known fact that honey forms a part of several ancient African rituals that are still followed by many

Africans to date.

Most African bees are disease free. Honey is generally a traditional and more often cottage industry leading to the production of unadulterated natural floral honey. In African culture, generally raw and natural honey is used. With some care and some modern techniques complementing traditional methods there is a high potential to develop honey from Africa not only as a sweetener but also as a potential medicine. This honey may then be used not only by traditional but also by more mainstream western medicine systems.

The African systems of medicine use honey to treat several conditions. Honey has been mostly used by healers from Africa to treat the several conditions including:

- Bed wetting in children
- To treat burns
- To control muscle cramps

## IN CHINESE MEDICINE SYSTEMS

Honey has formed a part of the daily diet of the Chinese from time immemorial. Shen Nang, belonging to the Xin dynasty, mentioned the importance of honey around 2000 BC. Writings from the Qin dynasty also commend the importance of honey.

Li Shi Zhen, a chemist from the Ming dynasty (1368-1644), in the text Compendium of Materia Medica gave a list of ailments that could be treated using honey and these included its use to remove heat, as a pain reliever and as a method of decreasing dehydration.

As part of its traditional medical systems, the Chinese use honey not as a sweetener but more for its medicinal properties. Although it is a neutral food, it is considered as having properties of enhancing yin (cold energy).

## As a Medicine

A teaspoon of honey mixed with milk, warm water or spread on bread is a part of the routine breakfast of many Chinese. Though a large amount of honey is exported from China there is a lot of honey consumed locally.

The Chinese use honey to treat the following conditions:
- To enhance yin
- To treat coughs and colds
- To fortify the spleen
- To clear allergies
- To prevent constipation
- To improve eyesight
- To treat anxiety
- To treat insomnia
- To treat gastritis
- To treat stomach ulcers.
- To cure indigestion
- To detoxify the body
- To reduce pain
- To relax and balance energy

# 10

# HONEY AND SPORTS AND GAMES

Honey is a natural carbohydrate that provides energy to the body in the form of calories. It is a natural and convenient energy boost. It can be used by athletes to enhance their performance and to increase their endurance. It is said that athletes especially runners used honey as an energy booster during the ancient Olympics that were held in ancient Greece.

Since sportspersons need extra energy both to train and perform, several studies have been carried out under the auspices of the National Honey Board. These studies have mainly compared the efficacy of honey in relation to other carbohydrates. The conclusion from these studies has proved that honey performed as well and better than other sources of carbohydrates.

In total three different studies: double, blind and placebo controlled, honey proved to be a good source of carbohydrate necessary for sportspersons. The studies were carried out at the Exercise and Sport Nutrition Laboratory at the University of Memphis by Dr Richard Kreider and his team.

- The first study involved 71 persons who were given one among seven different carbohydrates gels including honey and a placebo. It was found that honey did not bring on hypoglycemia. It produced very slight increases in insulin and blood sugar. It was found to be a little better when compared with maltodextrin and dextrose (glucose). It was similar in function to a commonly available commercial gel. Thus it was concluded that honey was a good source of carbohydrate for pre work out sessions.

- The second study involved 30 weight trainers both men and women. After an intensive workout these subjects were given a protein shake which had been blended with a carbohydrate source including maltodextrin, powdered honey, sucrose or a placebo. The powdered honey sweetened protein health drink showed the best result. It was the only milk shake that sustained the blood sugar for a period of two hours following the exercise.
- The third study involved 9 competitive cyclists. These cyclists were given a gel containing glucose, honey or a placebo at regular intervals; the first one prior to and the other ones at intervals of 10 miles for a total 40 mile simulated race. The results were very promising. The honey gel equalled the performance of glucose gel and showed a significant increase in both speed and performance over the placebo.

These three studies effectively demonstrated the role of Honey in sports. The first study confirmed that honey may be used as a "time released" fuel for exercising muscle. The second study shows that honey may be used as a good source of carbohydrate to replenish muscles. However, the third study showed the most promising results as it confirmed that honey can be used to improve endurance exercise. Thus honey with its low glycemic index, positive metabolic response and its effective production of energy can be used as a good carbohydrate source for sport.

# MEAD

Mead is an ancient fermented beverage that has found mention in both myths and legends. Considered as a drink of the Gods and humans it was attributed with possessing several magical powers both exaggerated and real.

In Europe, mead was used in rituals involving various ancient clans including Celts, Vikings and the Anglo Saxons. It was an integral part of their various ancient rituals. In fact the word honeymoon is said to be derived from the practice of a newlywed couple drinking mead for a whole month or a moon. If a boy was born nine months later credit was given to "mead" as there was a belief that mead improved fertility. Later, it lost popularity as other fermented beverages especially those made from grape and other fruits gained prominence.

Mead is made by the process of fermentation. Generally fermented beverages involve both technical expertise as well as experience. Making mead is considered both an art and a science. To manufacture basic mead, water and honey are fermented with yeast. There are various types of mead including traditional varieties and other varieties. Traditional mead contains only water and honey. In other formulation various ingredients may be added. Small amounts of other ingredients including spices, herbs, fruit juices etc and these may be added to make different types of mead. Acids, stabilizers and sulphites may also be added to improve the shelf life of mead.

Mead brandy may also be manufactured. This beverage is made by combining malted grain with honey. The resultant mead is distilled. To make a honey liqueur, extra honey may be added to mead brandy.

# 12

# HONEY-SAFETY AND ALLERGIC PROPERTIES

Honey is generally considered safe for children but may not be recommended by some countries for infants below the age of 12 months. Honey naturally contains spores of Clostridium botulinum. However the levels reported are quite low. Generally an adult or even a child has no problem with the presence of these spores in honey but the spores can survive theoretically in the stomach of infants below a year in age. Hence it is not recommended for use in infants.

Sometimes customs including Indian ones, where the first food given to infants is a drop of honey are followed quite commonly in many parts of India. No deaths have been reported but perhaps the infant deaths may not have been attributed to spores in honey. It is easier to claim that honey is safe for children above the age of one year and adults. It is indeed a fact that some studies have shown that infants tolerate honey better than sucrose. Other studies have shown that crying phase also decreased with the use of honey when compared with a placebo. Hence it is indeed difficult to draw a firm conclusion on how susceptible infants may be to honey and many cultures do permit the use of honey for infants below the age of one.

A very miniscule population may be allergic to honey or to pollen or beeswax or other honey related products. Honey anaphylaxis has been reported as a very rare occurrence.

# UNUSUAL USES OF HONEY AND HONEYBEES

## AS AN IMPLANT FILLER MATERIAL

Honey, being a natural compound and having natural wound healing properties has lent itself to unusual research. One of these research studies is the use of honey as an implant filler material.

Research studies on an experimental basis were conducted by a group of researchers to study the effects of using natural honey as implant filler in place of the commonly used silicone gel or sterile saline. Natural and sterile honey from beehives was used and the honey filled implants were studied. The following conclusions were the result: natural honey had more radiolucency when compared with silicone gels and a higher viscosity when compared with sterile saline. The honey filled implants were found to be biocompatible and caused lesser tissue reactions when compared with the silicone gel.

It is important that further studies should be conducted to assess long term benefits. However honey does show promise as an implant filler material.

## AS AN INDICATOR OF ENVIRONMENTAL POLLUTION

Some countries like the United States, the United Kingdom, Canada and Italy use Honeybees to keep an eye on environmental pollution. They measure the buildup of heavy metals and other pollutants in various hive products including honey and pollen. They also measure the heavy metal contaminations in the bees to study the impact of environment pollution.

# TRIVIA

Honey was traditionally used to make vinegar. Today specialty vinegars are sometimes made using honey and are very expensive.

Through history honey was bought in honey combs to ensure its purity and this practice is still followed by many even today.

The Honey Bee is the State Insect of New Jersey.

Ancient Egypt considered the honey bee as a symbol of health, wealth and power.

In 1973 Karl von Frisch received a Nobel Prize for deciphering the honey bees' stylish language of communication using unique dance movements.

A bee must consume between 6 to 8 lbs of honey to produce 1 lb of beeswax.

According to a Greek legend the wings with which Icarus and his father Deadalus flew, were supposed to be made of feathers glued together with beeswax. Icarus supposedly flew too close to the sun and his wings melted and he fell into the Aegean Sea and drowned.

The ancient God Pan was called the guardian of the bees. He made his legendary pipes joining reeds together using beeswax and produce celestial music.

Mythology speaks of Cupid dipping his arrows in honey before shooting them on unsuspecting victims who may just become the most fortunate people on earth when they fell in love.

September is National Honey Month in the US.

Bees must draw nectar from over 2 million flowers to produce 1 lb of honey and almost 6 million flowers to produce one kg of honey.

Bees generally fly a distance of one or two miles away from their hives but are capable of making a six mile journey.

There are over 300 varieties of flowers and trees from which bees collect honey.

Lighter coloured honeys are generally more expensive than darker coloured honeys.

Piero di Cosimo a Florentine renaissance artist painted **The Discovery of Honey** by Bacchus.

Lucas Cranach the Elder a German artist painted **Venus and Amor** as honey thieves.

Honey is most often used for breakfast on a slice of bread or as a sweetener for milk or tea.

Honey is produced by all the countries of the world. However the production time varies and may last for a few weeks in some countries whereas it is produced almost throughout the year in others.

Honey is almost always safe. However honey obtained from certain plants of the heath family is toxic. It is sometimes called "mad honey" and contains grayanotoxins, which are chemicals that can inhibit breathing and have a hypnotic effect.

Honey, in combination with orange juice and yogurt, is supposed to cure hangovers.

## REFERENCES

1. Doner, L.W. (1977) The sugars of honey-A review. Journal of the Science of Food and Agriculture, 28:443-456
2. Barhate R.S., Subramanian R., Nandini K.E., Umesh Hebbar H. Processing of honey using polymeric microfiltration and ultrafiltration membranes (2003) Journal of Food Engineering, 60 (1), November 2003 pp 49-56
3. Subramanian R., Hebbar H.U. Rastogi N.K. Processing of Honey: A Review International Journal of Food Properties Volume 10, Issue 1, January 2007, pages 127-143
4. Aykut Misirlioglu, Kaan Gideroglu, Tayfun Akoz and Aylin Ege Gul As an alternative filler material: natural honey (experimental study) European Journal of Plastic Surgery 2006 Volume 29, Number 1, 29-34
5. Cooper Rose A, and Jenkins Leighton A Comparison between Medical Grade Honey and Table Honeys in Relation to Antimicrobial Efficacy Wounds Issue: 21 (2) February 2009
6. Paul Ian M, Beiler Jessica, Mc Monagle Amyee, Shaffer Michele L, Duda Laura and Berlin Jr. Chester M. Effect of Honey, Dextromethorphan, and No Treatment on Nocturnal Cough and Sleep Quality for Coughing Children and Their Parents Arch Pediatr Adolesc Med. 2007;161(12): 1140-1146
7. Orla, Sherlock Anthony, Dolan Rahma, Athman Power Alice, Gethin Georgina, Cowman Sheamus and Humphreys Hilary Comparison of the antimicrobial activity of Ulmo honey from Chile and Manuka honey against methicillin-resistant Staphylococcus aureus, Escherichia coli and Pseudomonas aeruginosa BMC Complimentary and Alternative Medicine 2010, 10:47

8. Agbaje E. O., Ogunsanya T., Aiwerioba I. R., Conventional Use of Honey as an Antibacterial Agent Annals of African Medicine, Vol.5, No.2. 2006, pp. 78-81

## BIBLIOGRAPHY

1. Book of Honey Stefan Bogdanov Bee Product Science 2010
2. The Honey Prescription: The Amazing Power of Honey as Medicine Nathaniel Altman Inner Traditions Bear & Company 2010
3. The ABC and Xyz of Bee Culture: an encyclopedia pertaining to scientific and practical culture of bees By A.I. Root, E.I. Root Kessinger 2007

## WEBSITES

www.bee-hexagon.net
www.honey.com
www.honeyassociation.com
www.lrrd.org
www.unctad.org
www.sciencecentric.com
www.honeytraveler.com
www.wikipedia.com